RIPLEY's OCEANS

Believe It or Not!®

RIPLEY
PUBLISHING

a Jim Pattison Company

TWISTS

Written by Camilla de la Bedoyere
Consultant Barbara Taylor

RIPLEY PUBLISHING

Publisher Anne Marshall

Editorial Director Rebecca Miles
Project Editor Lisa Regan
Editorial Assistant Charlotte Howell
Picture Researchers James Proud, Charlotte Howell
Proofreader Judy Barratt
Indexer Hilary Bird

Art Director Sam South
Senior Designer Michelle Cannatella
Design Rocket Design (East Anglia) Ltd
Reprographics Juice Creative Ltd

www.ripleybooks.com

CONTENTS

WHAT'S INSIDE YOUR BOOK? 4

WILD WIND AND WAVES 6
WORLD WEATHER

OCEAN MOTION 8
OUT OF SIGHT

GROW ZONE 10
GOING COASTAL

ANIMALS IN ARMOR 12
SAFETY SUITS

GOOD REEF 14
COOL CORALS

PAGE 19

PAGE 24

TWISTS

HUNT OR HIDE 32
FEEDING TIME

PAGE 13

SUPERSIZE SEA 16
BIG IT UP

TOXIC SHOCK 34
RISK OF DEATH!

SOMETHING FISHY 18
MASTERS **OF THE SEA**

SMART MOVES 36
HERE WE GO

FAST, FURIOUS, FREAKY 20
BIODIVERSITY RULES OK

MARINE MYSTERIES 38
CASE STUDIES

PAGE 40

MEGAMOUTHS 22
SHARK ATTACK!

WATER WINGS 24
BIRDBRAINS

DEEP-SEA EXPLORERS 40
THAT SINKING FEELING

MARINE MAMMALS 26
ALL AT SEA

UP ANCHOR! 42
WAVE GOODBYE

LOOK AT ME 28
STEALING THE SHOW

TREASURE TROVE 44
WHAT'S IN STORE?

INTO THE ABYSS 30
DEEP AND DARK

INDEX 46

MAKING A SPLASH

Have you ever gazed out at the ocean and wondered what lies beneath? Well, wonder no more. Take an ocean trip without getting your hair wet, and dip a toe into the great sea of knowledge!

Two-thirds of our planet is water, and the five great oceans are full of more creatures than any other place on Earth. From the sunny shallows to the dark and dingy depths, this book will bring you face to face with marine mammals, deep sea divers, and lots and lots of fish. Come on… dive in!

WHAT'S INSIDE YOUR BOOK?

ALL CHANGE

This octopus is called the "day octopus" because it hunts in the day. As such it needs to be a camouflage expert, so it can hunt successfully, and not be hunted. It is usually brown but can change color as it swims from sand and rocks to coral. One marine biologist reported seeing an individual day octopus changing color and patterns 1,000 times in seven hours.

It is one of the largest octopus species, with tentacles 30 inches long.

Learn fab facts to go with the cool pictures.

The day octopus is sometimes called the big blue octopus.

Some colors allow "false eye" spots to be seen in its pattern, near its tentacles.

TWISTS

BLUE WHALE
The world's largest ever creature, a blue whale eats about 4 tons of krill (a tiny shrimplike sea creature) every day.
Size: 80–100 feet

THRESHER SHARK
A thresher shark can leap right out of the water. Its tail is often half the length of its body.
Size: 10–16½ feet

SEA LION
A California sea lion dives for up to five minutes, but can hunt non-stop for up to 30 hours.
Size: 5½–7¼ f

Ripley explains...

Ripley explains some of the science and know-how from oceanic experts.

GOOD REEF

COOL CORALS

Coral reefs lie in the shimmering blue waters of coastal areas. They make up just one percent of all ocean habitats, but these natural places are home to [per]cent of all marine animals and plants.

[Yo]u may think of a coral reef as a rocky [pla]ce underwater, but it is much more [th]an that. Inside each reef there are [mi]llions of mini-builders called polyps. [...] soft-bodied animals build rocky cups [...]d their soft bodies. Over thousands [of yea]rs, the cups create an enormous [stru]cture—the reef itself—and this [is] a giant ecosystem where a huge [...] of living things exist together.

BIG WORD ALERT

ECOSYSTEM
This is a place, such as a rainforest or coral reef, and includes all the animals and plants that live in it and interact with each other.

STACHORN CORAL

twist it!

Some types of coral can survive in deep, dark, and cold water. There may be more coldwater coral reefs than warm ones.

The most famous reef is the Great Barrier Reef in Australia's waters. It isn't actually just one reef, but a group of around 3,000 reefs and 1,000 small islands that spread nearly 1,250 miles.

Most coral polyps are colonial animals, which means they live together in big groups. They don't always get on, and if there is not much space one polyp might lean over and kill its next-door neighbor!

The Coral Triangle is a huge area of sea around Indonesia and Malaysia with many coral islands and reefs. More than 3,000 types of fish live there.

REEF RICHES

STAR CORAL

CORAL

BRAIN CORAL

FAN CORAL

[There a]re many [differe]nt types of [coral] and some of [them h]ave names [that d]escribe their [appea]rance perfectly!

FASCINATING FACT! FASCINATING FACT!

MUSHROOM CORAL

Ripley's Believe It or Not!

Coral kids

These figures are part of an underwater sculpture museum created by a London artist named Jason de Caires Taylor. Jason's artwork is designed to encourage the growth of new corals.

Look for the Ripley "R" to find out even more than you knew before!

These books are all about "Believe It or Not!"— amazing facts, feats, and things that will make you go "Wow!"

PELICAN

Pelicans can eat 2 pounds of fish each day and can swallow a fish that is 1½ feet long.

Size: 3⅓–6 feet

LOBSTER

The biggest lobster ever caught was nearly 4 feet long. It was caught in Nova Scotia, Canada, and was probably over 100 years old.

Size: up to 3¼ feet

SEAHORSE

Seahorses need to eat nearly all the time to stay alive. They have no teeth and no stomach.

Size: 0.6–14 inches

WILD WIND AND WAVES

WORLD WEATHER

Ever wondered where weather comes from, and if the weather, wind, waves, and warm air are all connected? The answer is yes! The world's weather is all down to the ways that the Sun, the Earth, its oceans, and the atmosphere work together.

Oceans are giant weather-makers and climate-shakers. They control the planet's atmosphere and temperature, and our seasons, winds, and rains. Ocean water collects heat around the Equator, and moves it as far as the Poles—keeping most of the world warm enough for living things to exist. Warm wet air collects over the oceans as clouds and travels to land, where it falls as rain.

<< Turn the tide >>

The way that ocean water can move closer to, or further away from a coastline is called a tide. Tides happen twice a day in most places and are caused by the way the Moon's gravity pulls on the Earth. In Nova Scotia, Canada, the difference between the ocean's depth at low tides and high tides can reach nearly 50 feet: that is the height of eight men standing on top of one another!

BIG WORD ALERT

ATMOSPHERE
The thick layer of gases, including the oxygen we breathe, that surrounds the Earth. The atmosphere plays a big part in the world's weather.

ALL AT SEA

- Waves are caused by wind moving the surface of the ocean. As they approach land, where the water gets shallow, waves move more slowly, but they can become taller.

- A wave at sea is called a swell and the largest ones ever measured reached over 100 feet from their troughs (bottoms) to their crests (tops).

- Broken wave patterns might mean deadly rip currents. These currents can pull even the strongest swimmers out to sea, so never swim without an adult's supervision.

Icebergs are giant blocks of floating ice that form in the cold polar regions. Oil companies use boats and ropes to move them when they want to explore the seafloor below!

Warm ocean water creates hurricanes by heating air. The warm air starts to swirl, creating winds that become giant storms. When they move onto land, hurricane winds, heavy rain, and a rapid rise in sea level (a storm surge) cause devastation in coastal areas. Hurricanes are also called tropical cyclones or typhoons in the western Pacific Ocean.

The middle of a hurricane is fairly calm and is called "the eye."

Ripley explains...

Cloud formation

Rain

Water vapor

Water runs back to the ocean

Ocean

THE WATER CYCLE

Oceans are a major part of the whole world's water system, which is called the global water cycle. Rainwater flows from land to the oceans, and when ocean water is heated it evaporates to form clouds.

OCEAN MOTION

OUT OF SIGHT

Beneath the gently slurping, swelling surface of the oceans, there is a whole other world waiting to be explored. Imagine you are about to dive all the way to the bottom of the sea... you're embarking on a perilous journey.

You travel through the light zones, where sunlight still reaches, and shoals of fish swim past. As you dive deeper, you notice the darkness, and the deathly cold and quiet around you. There are few signs of life. On the ocean floor, your feet sink into deep squashy mud and sludge.

BIG WORD ALERT

MARINE
This word is used to describe anything to do with seas and oceans.

Deep diver

William Trubridge is a top free-diver. In this extreme sport, people descend as far as they can below the surface of the sea on a single breath of air. In 2009, William reached a lung-crunching depth of 288 feet 8 inches.

Normal level

Water recedes

Tsunami hits

Tsunami power

These images show the movement of water during the 2004 Indian Ocean tsunami, at Kalutara in Sri Lanka. The top picture shows the normal level of the ocean. Then, just before the tsunami hit, the water pulled back from the shoreline, and then swirled across roads and houses. This tsunami killed over 200,000 people in 14 countries.

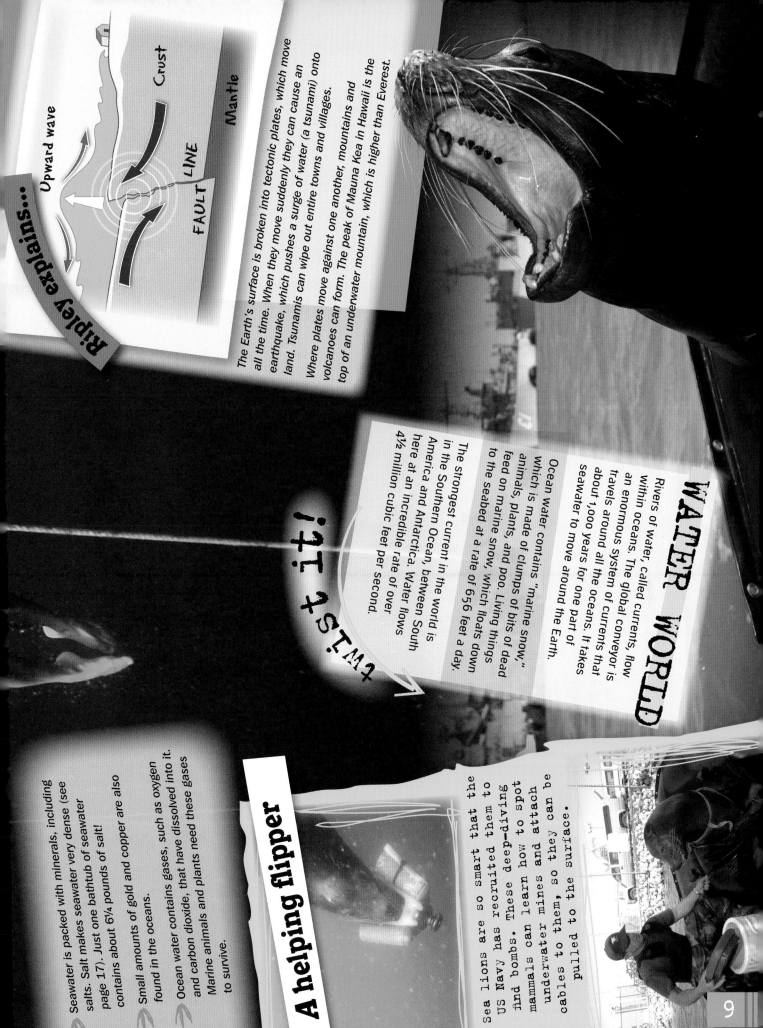

Ripley explains...

Upward wave

Crust

Mantle

FAULT LINE

The Earth's surface is broken into tectonic plates, which move all the time. When they move suddenly they can cause an earthquake, which pushes a surge of water (a tsunami) onto land. Tsunamis can wipe out entire towns and villages.

Where plates move against one another, mountains and volcanoes can form. The peak of Mauna Kea in Hawaii is the top of an underwater mountain, which is higher than Everest.

WATER WORLD

Rivers of water, called currents, flow within oceans. The global conveyor is an enormous system of currents that travels around all the oceans. It takes about 1,000 years for one part of seawater to move around the Earth.

Ocean water contains "marine snow," which is made of clumps of bits of dead animals, plants, and poo. Living things feed on marine snow, which floats down to the seabed at a rate of 656 feet a day.

The strongest current in the world is in the Southern Ocean, between South America and Antarctica. Water flows here at an incredible rate of over 4½ million cubic feet per second.

Twist it!

- Seawater is packed with minerals, including salts. Salt makes seawater very dense (see page 17). Just one bathtub of seawater contains about 6¼ pounds of salt!

- Small amounts of gold and copper are also found in the oceans.

- Ocean water contains gases, such as oxygen and carbon dioxide, that have dissolved into it. Marine animals and plants need these gases to survive.

A helping flipper

Sea lions are so smart that the US Navy has recruited them to attach them to the top of underwater mines and bombs. These deep-diving mammals can learn how to spot underwater mines and attach a buoy to them, so they can be pulled to the surface.

GROW ZONE
GOING COASTAL

As oceans are the world's biggest habitat it's no wonder they teem with life. There are more living things in ocean waters than anywhere else, and the biggest variety live near the surface.

The reasons for this are simple: in the top 650 feet of water (known as the Sunlight Zone) there is light, warmth, and plenty of food—what more could anyone ask for? This region is like the farms or rainforests of the oceans, where food for ocean animals grows. Shallow areas around land are called coasts and they are particularly busy places.

BIG WORD ALERT

HABITAT
The place where a plant or animal naturally lives and grows.

Marvelous mussels!

Rivers flow into the coastal areas, bringing lots of fresh water and food, making these places especially good habitats. Some coastal plants and animals, such as these mussels, have to be able to survive underwater, when the tide is in, and in air when the tide goes out.

First swim of the day, lovely!

Played hide and seek in the water

A DAY IN THE LIFE...

Sea otters like to snooze in coastal kelp forests because the seaweed stops them from floating away in their sleep. These marine animals are smart—they lie on their backs and use stones to smash open crabs and shells they have balanced on their bellies!

Met up with the gang. More swimming...

A shellfish snack while swimming.

Coast

Ocean

Continental shelf

Continental slope

TAKING A DIP

The continental shelf is where land slopes gently into the sea. Light can pass through the water here, right down to the seabed. That's why shallow areas in the sea are called the Sunlight Zone.

Little archer fish catch flying insects by spitting at them! When a stunned insect falls into the water, the smart fish gobbles it up.

GOTCHA!

Sea trees

In some warm places, mangrove trees grow along coasts to create mangrove swamps. Strangely, these trees don't mind salty seawater and they make unique habitats. More than half the world's mangrove swamps have been destroyed in recent times, to make room for fish and shrimp farms.

FEELING WEEDY

Seaweeds are not like other plants—they're slimy! The slime stops other animals from settling on them, and keeps them from drying out at low tide.

Tiny animals and plants, called plankton, drift along in the ocean's Sunlight Zone. They are the food of many other animals. A large whale can eat more than 5,000 pounds of plankton in a day.

We use seaweed as food and to make medicines, cosmetics (make-up), paint, glue, and paper.

Brown seaweeds are called kelp and they used to be burned to make soap. Kelp can grow as enormous underwater forests and some types can grow 1–2 feet a day.

twist it!

COASTAL CROCS

Gharials are slender-jawed relatives of crocodiles. They live in coastal waters around India, but they will probably be extinct in the wild soon. There are only about 200 left.

ANIMALS IN ARMOR

SAFETY SUITS

If you've got a soft, spongy body, what's the best way to protect yourself from predators? Many small marine animals have got the perfect answer—they wear armor. This armor is like a super-strong skin and it's packed with tough minerals that make it hard. A crustacean's armor is called a carapace, but mollusks grow shells.

Sea urchins and starfish hide their armor under a thin layer of colorful skin. They have skeletons made up of interlocking plates of calcium— the strong mineral that's in our bones and teeth. The animals in this group have their mouths on their bottoms and tiny suckers called feet!

COCONUT SHY

This veined octopus doesn't grow tough armor, so he made his own out of a coconut shell. He can close the shell when he wants to hide, but when it's time to make a quick getaway he grabs it with his eight tentacles, and runs for it!

Japanese giant

This colossal crustacean's Japanese name means "tall-leg." No prizes for guessing why! The largest Japanese spider crab ever recorded measured an enormous 145¼ inches from the tip of one leg to another. And some fishermen swear they've seen crabs that are nearly double that size!

twist it!

Scientists have copied their technique, and built a digging robot called RoboClam.

Razor clams can dig themselves into the seabed at a super-speedy rate of 1 inch every second.

When Paul Westlake lost his wallet in the ocean, he thought he'd seen the last of it. A few days later, however, a deep-sea diver found the missing wallet on the ocean floor, in the clutches of a large lobster!

Scaly-foot snails have ultra-tough armor. Their shells are so strong that scientists are studying them to find out how to make better armor for soldiers and vehicles. The secret lies in the snails' three-layer shells, which are strengthened with iron.

SO SHELLFISH

ARMY OF ARMS

Three five-armed starfish devour a dead fish. Like heavily armored tanks, the animals can munch away, protected from predators by their tough outer skins.

CRAB RACING

Meet the elite sports stars of the crab world. These hermit crabs have undergone thorough fitness training to reach their peak, and are primed and ready to race. These little athletes compete for the National Crab Racing Association, based in Florida, and after six months they retire in style, to spend their remaining days in the lap of luxury as pampered pets.

Watch out!

Sea urchins don't have eyes, which might be why this little guy didn't spot the giant sea snail approaching! Sea urchins have spiky spines, but they are still no match for this mighty mollusk.

GOOD REEF

COOL CORALS

Coral reefs lie in the shimmering blue waters of coastal areas. They make up just one percent of all ocean habitats, but these natural places are home to 25 percent of all marine animals and plants.

You may think of a coral reef as a rocky place underwater, but it is much more than that. Inside each reef there are millions of mini-builders called polyps. These soft-bodied animals build rocky cups around their soft bodies. Over thousands of years, the cups create an enormous, solid structure—the reef itself—and this becomes a giant ecosystem where a huge variety of living things exist together.

BIG WORD ALERT

ECOSYSTEM

This is a place, such as a rainforest or coral reef, and includes all the animals and plants that live in it and interact with each other.

STAR CORAL

FINGER CORAL

BRAIN CORAL

There are many different types of coral, and some of them have names that describe their appearance perfectly!

14

STAGHORN CORAL

Some types of coral can survive in deep, dark, and cold water. There may be more coldwater coral reefs than warm ones.

The most famous reef is the Great Barrier Reef in Australia's waters. It isn't actually just one reef, but a group of around 3,000 reefs and 1,000 small islands that spread nearly 1,250 miles.

Most coral polyps are colonial animals, which means they live together in big groups. They don't always get on, and if there is not much space one polyp might lean over and kill its next-door neighbor!

The Coral Triangle is a huge area of sea around Indonesia and Malaysia with many coral islands and reefs. More than 3,000 types of fish live there.

REEF RICHES

FAN CORAL

MUSHROOM CORAL

Ripley's Believe It or Not!®

Coral kids

These figures are part of an underwater sculpture museum created by a London artist named Jason de Caires Taylor. Jason's artwork is designed to encourage the growth of new corals.

SUPERSIZE SEA

BIG IT UP

Enormous eye

The colossal squid of the Southern Ocean has the biggest eyes of any living animal. Each eyeball can measure nearly 10 inches across and—no surprises here—it has fantastic eyesight, even though it can't see anything in color.

In 2007, fishermen in the Antarctic seas caught a colossal squid that was 33 feet long and weighed nearly 1,000 pounds. That's more than twice the weight of a large male gorilla.

ACTUAL SIZE!

almost 10 inches wide!

When it comes to surviving undersea, size really matters. Being big has one major advantage—it's much harder for other things to catch and eat you!

Seawater is denser than freshwater, or air. That means the particles, or molecules, inside it are packed tightly together, and can hold up objects in it. That's why we can float quite easily in seawater. Things feel lighter in seawater than they do in air, because the water pushes up underneath them and supports their weight. That means ocean animals can grow much bigger than those on land. Floating in seawater may be easy, but moving through it takes lots of energy. So, marine monsters often travel with ocean currents.

Ripley's Believe It or Not!®

The oceans are full of worms that burrow into the seafloor, or live inside another animal. The longest in the world are boot-lace worms, which live in the North Sea. They can grow to 100 feet long!

Mega yuck!

Giant clam

Giant clams can measure more than 3 feet across. They live around coral reefs and get food from the water, or from tiny algae that live on the edges of their shells. It is thought they can live to 100 years of age, or even longer.

BIG BLUE BABY

A blue whale calf is one-and-a-half times the length of an average-sized car when it is born. Blue whales are the world's largest animals, so it's no wonder they have big bouncing babies! They weigh up to 3 tons at birth—that's the same as 882 human newborns. Once born, the baby (which is known as a calf) drinks over 400 pints of its mother's milk every day.

Blue whales produce monster-sized pink poo! Each poo is nearly 10 inches wide and many feet long! The strange color comes from krill, the little shrimp-like animals the whales eat.

FASCINATING FACT! FASCINATING FACT!

17

What's in a name?

Some fish get their names from the way they look. Would you kiss one of these—even if it was called "sweetlips"?

ANGEL FISH

HARLEQUIN SWEETLIPS

MASKED BUTTERFLY FISH

SOMETHING FISHY

MASTERS **OF THE SEA**

Fish have been around for a very long time: for more than 500 million years! The oceans and seas are now home to zillions of them, and there are more fish in the world than any other type of vertebrate.

Fish are the masters of the sea, but what's the secret to their success? Being able to breathe underwater has got to be one big advantage! A backbone helps, too—it gives an animal something to build its muscles and organs around, and connects the brain to all the other body bits. Fish were the first creatures on Earth to develop a backbone, and it was so successful that all of us other vertebrates then copied this brilliant design.

BIG WORD ALERT

VERTEBRATE
An animal with a backbone. Fish, birds, reptiles, amphibians, and mammals are vertebrates.

School meals

The super-talented sailfish has an amazing way of dining out. Several of smaller fish, like sardines or anchovies, into a "baitball," and then use their high fins to create a wall to stop their prey from escaping.

PARROT FISH

PINEAPPLE FISH

TRUMPETFISH

Ripley's Believe It or Not!®

FAT FISH

The small fish at the top is an aptly named "great swallower" fish. It was found in the Cayman Islands having somehow eaten a snake mackerel five times bigger!

A fish's body is suited for life underwater. That usually means a body shape that is streamlined (the best shape for swimming), with just fins and tails.

Clowning around

All fish, including these clownfish, can breathe because they have special organs called gills, which take dissolved oxygen out of the water.

TOO COOL FOR SCHOOL

A group of fish is called a school or shoal. Millions of herrings get together to make giant, swarming shoals when it is time to spawn (lay their eggs). It's often safer to travel in a group!

Orange roughies don't look remarkable, but these deep-sea swimmers have been known to live to well over 100 years old—making them one of the longest-lived of all fish.

A group of eels is called a seething, a group of herrings is called an army, and a group of sharks is called a shiver.

Many fish have swim bladders that stop them from sinking. When gas goes into a swim bladder, the fish can move up in the water; when gas passes out of it, the fish can sink deeper.

TWIST A TAIL!

FAST, FURIOUS, FREAKY

BIODIVERSITY RULES OK

From flesh-sucking lampreys to four-eyed ghostly spookfish, there is an enormous range of fish in our oceans.

There are fish to suit almost every habitat, from rock pools at the seaside to the dark depths, and every way of life. There are hiders and fighters, swimmers and flyers, flat fish and fat fish, angry fish and clown fish—there are even fish with giant fangs, enormous mouths, or poisonous spines. There are also some frankly weird fish out there, too.

Fast!

WATCH OUT!

What a sucker!

This lovely lamprey is like a long, bendy hosepipe, with a scrubbing brush at the end. It attaches itself to its prey with a sucker-mouth while rows of tiny rasping teeth scrape away at the flesh. This hungry fella then sucks it up, with a side order of oozing blood. Yum!

Hey, suckers!

Barracudas are big (up to 6 feet in length) and they are smart. They chase their prey into shallow water and start to feed. Once they are full, the barracudas save the rest for later. They work together to guard their prey and stop them escaping!

Eating barracudas is a risky business, because they eat fish that feed on poisonous algae. If you feast on an affected fish you could suffer deadly food poisoning.

WHO YOU LOOKING AT?

Male garibaldis are furious little fish, with bad tempers. They grind their teeth and have been known to attack divers! If there are too many males in a group, some of them change into females.

Furious!

WEIRD AND WONDERFUL

Titan triggerfish don't like people one bit. These large fish attack divers and have a poisonous bite. They've even walloped divers so hard they've passed out!

Tuna fish never stop swimming. They keep moving at a rate of around 4 miles an hour for their entire lives. A 15-year-old tuna has probably swum about half a million miles!

When a female jawfish has laid her eggs, she scoots off and leaves the dad to take over. He keeps them in his mouth until they are ready to hatch.

Baby halibut look perfectly normal, but they morph into freaky flatfish as they grow. One eye moves across its head and joins the other one on the right-hand side, which becomes its head side. The mouth twists round to the fish's left side, which turns into its underbelly.

Twist it!

MR BLOBBY

Meet the blobfish: blob by name and slob by nature! These soft and squidgy creatures live in the deep waters around Australia, and they like a lazy life. Females sit on the ocean floor when protecting their eggs, but the rest of the time blobfish hover just above the seabed, mooching around and waiting for lunch to pass by.

Freaky!

Ripley's Believe It or Not!®

Up, up, and away!

Flying fish escape predators by leaping out of the water and gliding just above the waves. They can travel through the air for up to 40 seconds and cover around 150 feet.

MEGAMOUTHS

SHARK ATTACK!

Of all the world's creatures, sharks are among the most feared. Their incredible speed, cold black eyes, and rows of killer teeth set in enormous jaws have these sleek swimmers marked out as terrifying predators.

SOME-FIN SPECIAL

The megamouth is really a type of shark. It has a huge mouth, but eats tiny creatures such as plankton and jellyfish.

The smallest sharks are dwarf lantern sharks, which are usually 6–7 inches long.

A shark's body is covered in teeth rather than scales! Denticles are growths from the skin that are made of enamel (the same hard substance that's in teeth).

Tiger sharks eat almost anything: fish, squid, sea snakes, seals, birds, and stingrays... they have also been found with old tires, trash, and car license plates in their stomachs!

twist it!

Ripley explains...

Sharks usually have dark backs. This camouflages them against the dark water when seen from above. They are pale underneath, which helps them to remain invisible when viewed from below, against a pale sky. The same type of coloring is used in fighter planes.

Whale shark

Whale sharks are the largest fish in the world and can grow to over 40 feet long. They feed on tiny animals by opening their enormous mouths and sucking in water and food. This means that, if one swims near you, it's safe to stop and enjoy the view! In fact, as far as most sharks are concerned, you wouldn't make good grub. Nearly all sharks have no interest in attacking and eating humans.

We may fear sharks, but the truth is we know very little about them. There could be more than 500 different types of shark, with many of those still waiting to be discovered in the depths of the ocean. Lots of sharks are hunters, but the largest ones actually feed on shoals of tiny krill and other small animals. While some lay eggs, a few sharks are able to give birth to live young.

TOP 5 KILLER SHARKS

1. Great white
2. Tiger
3. Bull
4. Requiem
5. Sandtiger

TOP 3 SURVIVAL TIPS

Fight back: punch the shark on the snout—hard!

Stick your fingers in its eyes and gills.

Get out of the water!

Sharks, skates, and rays don't have bones—their skeletons are made of cartilage instead. Cartilage is more flexible than bone, and it's the same stuff that makes your nose and ears stiff.

Ripley's Believe It or Not!®

Life saver

Free diver Craig Clasen had to wrestle with a 12-foot tiger shark to save the life of his friend Ryan. An experienced diver, he recognized that the shark was hungry and highly dangerous. It took him two hours to fight off the shark, and he even tried to drown it.

Great white shark

- Baby great white sharks measure about 5 feet when they're born.
- A baby must leave its mother straightaway or it might get eaten!
- An adult can swim up to 25 mph.
- Great white sharks can vomit up their entire stomachs. It's a good way to clear out rubbish and bones and avoid an upset tummy!

23

WATER WINGS

Some birds swoop and soar over the oceans for months at a time. Others prefer to paddle at the seaside, pecking at tasty worms and shellfish. Penguins, however, are supreme marine birds—they are so well suited to ocean life that they have even lost the power of flight, and use their wings like flippers instead.

BLUE SHOES

This little fella is a little blue penguin called Elvis—and he's got blue shoes! He lives at the International Antarctic Centre in Christchurch, New Zealand, with several of his friends, who all wear shoes to protect their feet. They have developed sore feet after standing around much more than they would do in the wild, where they swim almost constantly.

SUN SUIT

Pierre the African penguin has his own wet suit! His friends at the California Academy of Sciences in San Francisco gradually lose their feathers to grow shiny new ones, but Pierre loses so many that he needs his suit to keep him warm, and to stop him from getting sunburn.

Watch the birdie

Marine birds have bodies suited for swimming and diving. Many have webbed feet, waterproof feathers, and special glands that help them deal with salt. Some birds fly over water, diving into the oceans to grab food. Others live on the coasts and feed on animals living in muddy seashores.

Male blue-footed boobies strut around in front of females, showing off their lovely webbed toes. The brighter the blue, the more the females are impressed!

Common guillemots lay eggs with very pointed ends. This shape stops the eggs from rolling off the cliff edges where the birds nest.

Herring gulls can be aggressive, and have been known to attack people and dogs.

BLUE-FOOTED BOOBIE

COMMON GUILLEMOT

HERRING GULL

The oceans contain fish, so it's no wonder that birds have adapted to be able to pluck these protein-packed snacks out of the salty water. No birds, however, have been able to become totally marine animals, because they all have to return to land to lay their eggs.

....WOW!

Wandering albatrosses have the biggest wingspan of any bird: 11½ feet—that's longer than two adult bikes! They live at sea, snatching squid from the water, and can fly for several weeks at a time without ever landing.

CATCH A WAVE

Surfing is a real action sport, and it's even better when you don't need a board! Gentoo penguins in the Falkland Islands know just where to go to get the best waves, and surf barefoot into shore. They even swim back out again to have another turn!

Ripley's—— **Believe It or Not!**®

Pelicans have enormous throat pouches, which they use to scoop up water: as much as 3 gallons at a time. They tip their heads back to drain out the water, and gobble up any fish.

Puffins are sometimes called sea parrots, because of their startling appearance. They spend most of their time at sea, occasionally diving to grab small fish.

Skuas have gross eating habits. They chase other sea birds and scare them into vomiting up their food—which the skuas then gobble up!

PELICAN

PUFFIN

SKUA

MARINE MAMMALS

ALL AT SEA

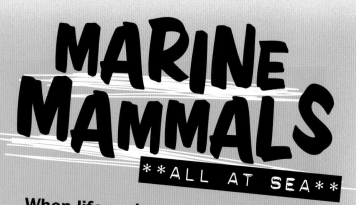

When life on land got too tough, some mammals headed back to the water. Whales, dolphins, seals, walruses, and dugongs are all descended from land-living beasts that decided, millions of years ago, that swimming is more fun than walking!

This devotion to the ocean was handy, because it meant marine mammals were able to escape from their predators, and find new sources of food: fish, krill, or seagrass. There were some major downsides though—they still had to breathe air, and life in water required new body shapes, less fur, and better ways to keep warm in the icy depths.

Polar bears

Polar bears have super-sensitive hearing and can detect seals swimming below ice that is 3-feet thick! Their sense of smell is impressive too—these giant bears can sniff the whiff of rotting meat 3 miles away. They dive into the water and bear-paddle their way to find lunch. They can swim for 60 miles without stopping!

KEY FACTS

- All marine mammals breathe air, but they have evolved (changed over time) to spend a long time underwater before needing to breathe again.

- Whales, dolphins, and porpoises belong to a group of mammals called cetaceans (say: set-aysh-uns). They give birth underwater and usually have just one baby at a time.

- The skeletons of marine mammals show they are descended from land-living animals that had four limbs.

Walrus

Male walruses can grow enormous teeth (called tusks) of 20 inches or more. They use the tusks to pull themselves onto slabs of ice and as lethal weapons when they fight one another.

Marine mammals may not be covered in fur, but they do have some sprouts of hair, such as whiskers. Young marine mammals usually have more hair than adults.

DOLPHINS

Dolphins play bubble hoopla! These clever creatures can create bubbles with air from their blowholes and swim through them. They like to make different shapes and sizes—just for fun!

Swimmers are sometimes surprised to find themselves surrounded by dolphins slapping their tails and circling. The dolphins aren't just being friendly—they are keeping prowling sharks away. No one knows why dolphins protect humans in this way.

twist it!

A blue whale's tongue weighs as much as a whole elephant!

Beluga whales are called sea canaries because they sing so sweetly.

Cetaceans are smart and can talk to each other. Humpback whales make the longest, most complicated sounds of any animal. They sing by forcing air through their nose.

Cetaceans and seals swim with their muscular tails, while sea lions use their front flippers.

IN THE SWIM

Elephant seals

Elephant seals can dive to depths of more than 3,000 feet and can wait for two hours between breaths. Their hearts beat very slowly when they dive, to save energy.

BIG
WORD ALERT

MAMMAL

These animals have hair or fur and give birth to live young, which they feed with their own milk.

LOOK AT ME

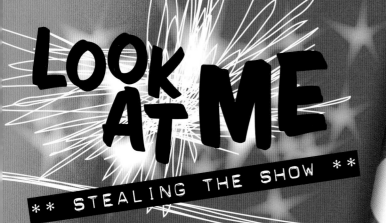

** STEALING THE SHOW **

There's an underwater beauty parade of animals that like to razzle, dazzle, dance, and display. Animals living in the Sunlight Zone (see page 10) get the full benefit of being in the spotlight, so they are more likely to show off with extraordinary colors and patterns than those who live in deeper, darker water. Light rays dance off their shimmering scales, patterned skins, and colored shells—what a sight!

Attention-seekers use their good looks to impress mates, or to warn predators to stay away. The shy and retiring types prefer to dress down and use colors and patterns to hide in dappled, shallow waters.

Harlequin shrimp

Some shrimps can change color to blend in with their surroundings, but harlequin shrimps are already perfec Their brightly colored patches may not look like an ideal type of camouflage, but when they are hidden i the shadows, the patterns help disguise the shrimp': outline. The harlequin shrimps then emerge to attac starfish, which they catch and eat alive, arm by arm

Mandarin fish are among the most beautiful of all reef fish, but their glorious neon colors are not there to impress. They warn potential predators of a foul-tasting slime that covers the fish's body.

MANDARIN FISH

Seafood salad

What would you call a crab that looks like a strawberry? A strawberry crab, of course! This tasty-looking fella has only been recently discovered, off the coast of Taiwan. Scientists are trying to find out why a crab would want to look like a strawberry. If they can find others that look like grapes, bananas, and oranges they plan to make a delicious crab fruit salad!

Ripley's Believe It or Not!®

CANDY FLATWORM

Some sea creatures like bold and brash looks, while others prefer the delicate and dainty approach. Candy flatworms hide their gentle beauty under rocks, until it's time to brave the waters and seek food. They glide smoothly along the seabed, or swim just above it.

Isn't this jellyfish gorgeous, with its lovely floaty body, pretty color, and little spots? At night these mauve stingers become even more attractive, because their bodies pulse with light as they are carried along by the currents. They may be good-looking, but these are jellyfish you wouldn't want to bump into—they are covered in stinging cells!

Color is created by pigments, which are in the outer layer of the animal's body. This outer layer may be skin, scales, or tough shells. Some deep-sea marine animals have colorful bacteria on their skin, or bacteria that produce light, for an extra-special spectacle.

I can't believe you're wearing the same as me tonight!

BIG
WORD ALERT

CAMOUFLAGE
The way an animal uses color and patterns to hide.

Dragon moray eels may have splendid colors, stripes, and spots, but they like to keep their beauty well hidden. They lurk in the shadows, and come out only at night.

INTO THE ABYSS

DEEP AND *DARK*

This habitat is so hostile that humans can only travel here in submersibles. So far, just two brave explorers have ever reached the deep ocean floor 6¾ miles down—that's fewer than have been to the Moon and back! This underwater world is not empty of life, though. Weird and wonderful creatures have made a home in the depths. Many of them feed on marine snow (see page 9) and the remains of dead animals that have sunk to the seabed.

If you could swim to the deepest parts of the ocean, you would be squashed to death in an instant by the huge weight of water above and around you. Sunlight can't reach the deep, and an eerie gloom takes over in the inky darkness.

BIG WORD ALERT

BIOLUMINESCENCE

(Say: bio—loom—in—ess—ence) Some animals can create their own light, either by using chemicals in their body or by covering themselves in light—producing bacteria. This is called bioluminescence. This is

Ooh, what big eyes you have
—all the better to see you with!

Spookfish

It's hard to see what's going on above you in the dark. Spookfish overcome this problem by combining eyes with mirrors and see-through heads! The fish dart upward eyes with mirrors and see-through heads! The fish can dart upward look out for shadows above, and can dart upward to catch prey they spy swimming overhead.

Red shrimp

Most deep-sea animals cannot see the color red, so this shrimp is actually invisible to them!

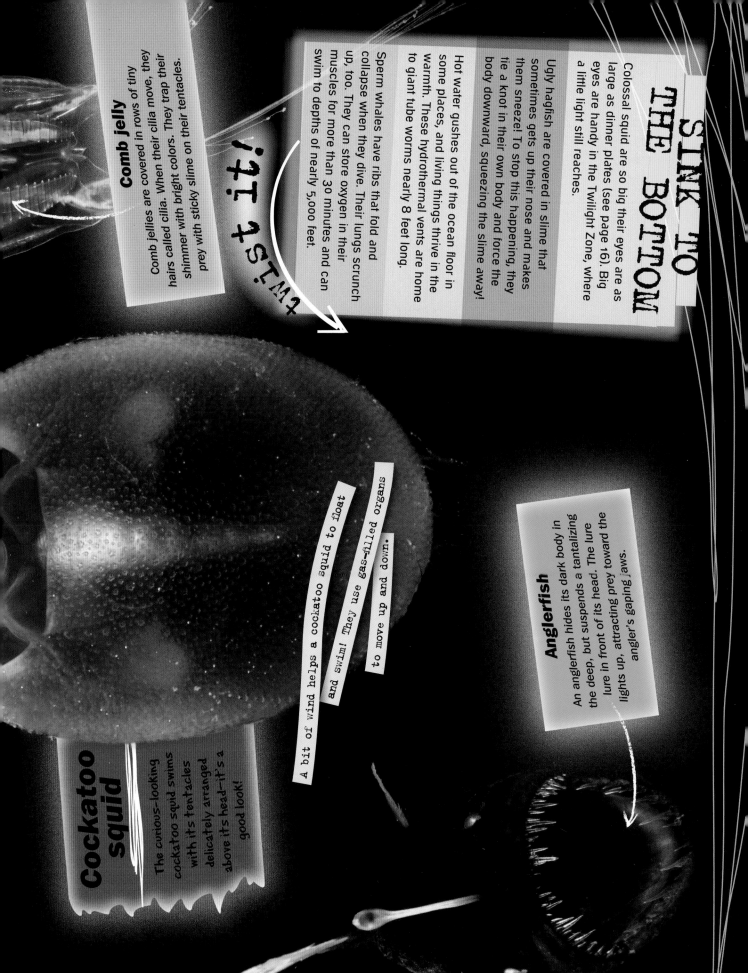

SINK TO THE BOTTOM

Colossal squid are so big their eyes are as large as dinner plates (see page 16). Big eyes are handy in the Twilight Zone, where a little light still reaches.

Ugly hagfish are covered in slime that sometimes gets up their nose and makes them sneeze! To stop this happening, they tie a knot in their own body and force the body downward, squeezing the slime away!

Hot water gushes out of the ocean floor in some places, and living things thrive in the warmth. These hydrothermal vents are home to giant tube worms nearly 8 feet long.

Sperm whales have ribs that fold and collapse when they dive. Their lungs scrunch up, too. They can store oxygen in their muscles for more than 30 minutes and can swim to depths of nearly 5,000 feet.

twist it!

Comb jelly

Comb jellies are covered in rows of tiny hairs called cilia. When their cilia move, they shimmer with bright colors. They trap their prey with sticky slime on their tentacles.

Cockatoo squid

The curious-looking cockatoo squid swims with its tentacles delicately arranged above its head—it's a good look!

A bit of wind helps a cockatoo squid to move to other organs and swim up and down. They use gas-filled

Anglerfish

An anglerfish hides its dark body in the deep, but suspends a tantalizing lure in front of its head. The lure lights up, attracting prey toward the angler's gaping jaws.

HUNT OR HIDE

HIDE

Food is energy—energy to grow, move, mate, and have young, and to eat even more food! Marine animals, just like those on land, have to spend lots of their time finding food. They also have to try their best not to become someone else's meal!

Animals that hunt others are called predators. They mostly need strength, speed, and great senses to find food. The lunch-bunch that get eaten are called prey, and their job is to hide, fight back, or fool predators into thinking they are something else completely. These crafty creatures have got some clever strategies up their sleeves!

Power puff

When a porcupine fish is scared, it hides in caves. If there's nowhere to hide, it fills its body up with water and swells to the size of a prickly football.

HIDE

Wolf fish

This ferocious-looking fish is called a wolf fish, because of its dog-like teeth. It lurks in dark corners and emerges only when it is hungry. Wolf fish like to exercise their jaws on crunchy shellfish, crabs, and sea urchins. Every year they grow new teeth to replace the ones destroyed by all that munching.

HUNT

Leaf me alone

Leafy seadragons are masters of disguise. These freaky-looking fish have frills that fool other animals into thinking they are seaweed. They move slowly, sucking prey into their straw-like mouths.

PICK UP A PENGUIN

Look who's come for tea! A killer whale has dropped by for a feast—a tasty penguin snack! These mighty mammals can flip blocks of ice over, so penguins are caught unawares and seals are and fall off!

Sargassum fish look just like seaweed. They lie in wait for crustaceans and small fish, although they have been known to eat fish as big as themselves!

Peculiar-looking cuttlefish can create flashes of color to dazzle their predators, or change color to blend in with their surroundings. If all that fails, these mollusks can disappear in a cloud of ink.

A saltwater crocodile can swim far out to sea. It grabs its prey with teeth that grow over 5 inches long, and holds it underwater until it drowns.

Shoals of mackerel fish dart, twist, and turn together in a group. Their scales reflect light so that confused predators can't pick out a victim among the swirling, twinkling bodies.

HIDE AND SEEK

Ripley's—— Believe It or Not!®

Fighting friends

Boxer crabs are the ocean's tough guys with a secret weapon that keeps them safe from predators: poisonous boxing gloves! These smart crustaceans grab hold of sea anemones in their claws and wave them around threateningly. Sea anemones have nasty stings, so predators keep clear of their tentacles. The sea anemones benefit from this strange friendship, too—crabs are such messy eaters they can collect crumbs and other bits of debris that fall out of the crab's mouth!

HIDE

Razor sharp

Razorfish swim in groups, upside down, with their heads pointing toward the seafloor. They look more like plants than predators.

Killer whales have teeth that are up to 4 inches long.

HUNT

Killer whales are smart—they hunt in family groups and can talk to one another in high-pitched sounds.

33

TOXIC SHOCK

A single taste of vile venom could be enough to kill you. Venom is poison that many animals have inside their bodies. It's a handy weapon in the fight to stay alive, but only if potential predators know you're carrying it around.

That's why many venomous animals like to advertise their highly toxic state with strong signals. Bright and bold colors, patterns, and spines all tell predators to keep a safe distance. Some predators, however, use venom to kill their prey. They like to keep their weapon of fast destruction under wraps until the last moment...

DEADLY ANEMONE

Sea anemones are related to jellyfish and, like their swimming cousins, they have stinging tentacles that contain venom. The venom is mostly used to stun or kill prey, but these animals also sting in self-defence.

POISON EATERS

Smart **sea slugs**, called nudibranchs, get their venom from the food they eat. They munch on poisonous corals, sponges, and sea anemones, and keep the venom or stings for themselves. Sea slugs wear bright colors to advertise their toxic skin.

STONY GROUND

Watch where you put your foot if you paddle in the warm clear waters of Southeast Asia. **Stonefish** lurk, hidden from view, on the seabed. They have venomous spines on their dorsal fins and they are the world's deadliest venomous fish.

BIG
WORD ALERT

TOXINS

Toxins, like poisons or venoms, are harmful. Something that contains toxins is described as toxic.

VENOMOUS SNAKE

A **beaked sea snake** is twice as deadly as any land snakes and has enough venom to kill 50 people. These swimming slitherers live in shallow water and are camouflaged, so humans often disturb them by accident.

GROUP OF KILLERS

A **Portuguese man o' war** may look like just one animal, but actually it's a whole colony of tiny stinging creatures that hang beneath a gas-filled balloon.

ROAR!

Don't ever square up to a **lionfish**. These brave animals have been known to attack humans, although they usually hunt small fish at night. One smack with a venomous spine is enough to stun the prey, so the lionfish can devour it.

SMART MOVES

Seawater is 830 times denser than air, and that makes moving through it quite an achievement. It's an effort that's worth making, though, as swimmers can go to new ocean locations, in search of food and mates.

Swimmers need lots of energy to get anywhere, which is why lots of marine animals just hang about instead! Many sea creatures are able to float in the ocean, or move up and down by controlling the amount of gas in their body. Others just go with the flow, and allow the sea currents to carry them to new places.

Slow motion

Maned seahorses are named after their lion-like mane of spines, but these fish don't have the big cat's speed. Seahorses have so little muscle power that they can scarcely swim at all and have to wrap their tail around seaweed, to stop any small current from carrying them away.

BIG WORD ALERT

DENSITY

The way that particles are packed inside a substance is called its density, and it is similar to weight. Water is denser, and heavier, than air.

The world's largest movement of animals—a migration—happens twice a day, every day, in the oceans. Under the cover of darkness, billions and billions of plankton swim up to the Sunlight Zone to feast on the tiny plants that grow there. When the sun rises, they swim back down to the Twilight or Dark Zones, and hide from predators.

FASCINATING FACT! FASCINATING FACT!

Hold on!

Every year, thousands of spiny lobsters grab hold of their friends in front to make one enormous line of marching crustaceans on the seabed. Each winter they migrate to deeper water—which is warmer and calmer than the shallow water near the shore at this time—to lay their eggs.

Fast forward

Sailfish can grow up to 11 feet long.

Sailfish are the fastest swimmers in the world.

They eat squid, octopus, and smaller fish such as sardines and anchovies.

They can reach speeds of 68 mph.

twist it!

WHAT A DRAG!

When an animal moves through water, the water particles push against it. This is called drag, and it slows movement right down.

Most sharks are slow swimmers, but the ferocious mako shark reaches top speeds of 55 mph.

Leatherback turtles are amazing long-distance swimmers. Using satellite-tracking systems, scientists discovered one turtle had swum 12,774 miles in a single migration!

Coconuts that fall into the sea can travel thousands of miles before coming to shore, where they might grow into new palm trees.

Deep sea lantern fish swim about a mile every night in a journey to the Sunlight Zone and back. That's like us running one-and-a-half marathons!

MOVE IT

SPEED LIMITS

Killer whale
34 mph

These enormous mammals can chase and kill animals even bigger than themselves.

California sea lion
25 mph

Fish swim fast, so sea lions need to be speedy to keep up with their lunch.

Gentoo penguins
23 mph

These birds almost fly underwater in short bursts when they are chasing their fishy prey.

37

MARINE MYSTERIES

Sailors, fishermen, swimmers, and explorers have all had good reason to fear the deep oceans. Far beneath the twinkling, rippling surface there could be all sorts of dangers, demons, or monsters lurking!

For thousands of years, people have reported spooky sounds, unexplained shipwrecks, and unrecognizable giant beasts at sea. Until recent times, it has been almost impossible to explore the underwater world, so people made up stories to explain any strange phenomena they encountered. There are usually good explanations for marine mysteries, but this huge habitat still holds many secrets.

MERMAIDS

The myth of mermaids has existed for thousands of years—even the great explorer Christopher Columbus believed he had seen several of them during his voyages. A mermaid is said to have the upper body of a woman, and the lower body of a fish. It's possible that this myth arose after people saw marine mammals, such as dugongs and manatees, from a distance.

HOAX

Dr. J. Griffin pretended he got this small "mermaid" from Japanese fishermen when he brought it to New York in 1842. Crowds of curious visitors paid 25 cents each to see the marvel. Is it real or a fake?

BIG WORD ALERT

CRYPTOZOOLOGIST
(say: Krip-toe-zoo-olo-jist)
People who study stories of mysterious animals, such as Krakens (huge mythical sea monsters), and hope to find the truth behind the tales.

INVESTIGATOR'S REPORT
Date: April 1918

Despite extensive searches, we are unable to find any sign of the USS Cyclops. This US Navy boat was lost at sea last month in a region known as the Bermuda Triangle, where other craft have mysteriously disappeared.

LOSSES: The whole crew (309 souls) is presumed lost at sea.

CAUSE: We are unable to establish cause of the disappearance of the ship. There is no wreckage and no distress signals were made.

CONCLUSION: The ship may have been bombed by wartime enemies, or sunk during a storm. However, there is no evidence to support either conclusion.

UNSOLVED

INVESTIGATOR'S REPORT
Date: January 1948

A Douglas DC-3 aircraft disappeared en route from Puerto Rico to Miami, passing through the Bermuda Triangle.

LOSSES: All 32 people on board are missing, presumed dead.

CAUSE: With no wreckage, and no survivors, it is impossible to say what caused the disappearance of the aircraft.

CONCLUSION: The pilot may not have received radio messages about a change in wind direction, causing him to get lost. Maybe he landed somewhere else safely? We will have to wait and see...

SOLVED

BLISTERING BARNACLES!

Something resembling a giant tentacled sea worm, more than 6 feet in length, alarmed locals when it washed ashore in Wales, UK, in 2009. Was it a mysterious marine monster that had been thrown up from the depths?

No, it actually turned out to be an unusually large colony of goose barnacles attached to an old ship's mast.

MYSTERY

SEA MONSTER

The following excerpt is taken from the diary of Jim Harris, a cabin boy on board HMS *Poseidon* in 1827. Does it prove the existence of sea monsters?

"Today we survived a most fearsome attack. The waves were billowing and the ship was pitching from side to side, when the Captain called all hands to deck. What a sight met our sorry eyes! A giant beast, the like of which I've never seen before, had grasped our vessel in its enormous tentacles, and threw us about like a leaf on a pond. We thought we were all done for. Suddenly, the heavens opened and a sheet of lightning ripped through the sky. The monster, which was most surely a kraken, took fright and fell beneath the waves. The Captain called us altogether for prayers of thanksgiving, but I'm too frightened to sleep tonight."

49

Ones to watch

bloop (noun)
Noise made by an unknown marine animal, first recorded underwater in 1997; no one has ever discovered what made them

globster (noun)
Dead body of an unidentified monster-like animal washed up on the shore; most globsters are big, jelly-like lumps and some are said to have shaggy hair

Kraken (noun, mythological)
Said to be enormous sea monsters that resemble squid or octopuses and live in the seas near Norway and Iceland

Longman's beaked whale (noun)
Regarded as the world's most mysterious whale—until recently, no living ones had ever been seen, and scientists only knew they existed because two skulls had been found

Red Devils (noun)
Once believed to be evil sea monsters by Mexican fishermen; have since been shown to be jumbo squid that dart through the water at lightning speed, and instantly change color from white to red when chased

DEEP-SEA EXPLORERS

THAT SINKING FEELING

For many explorers, the deep oceans present the world's last—and greatest—challenge. Every year, more people scale Mount Everest than climb into submarines to descend into the Abyss (see page 30).

Braving the depths is tough. Divers and explorers have to overcome a lack of oxygen, cold currents, and the weight of water bearing down on them.

Anyone wanting to go beyond a few hundred yards down needs to climb aboard an underwater vessel. It's a dangerous journey, but one that is rewarded by sights of incredible creatures. Are you ready to take the plunge?

In the 1940s, French diver Jacques Cousteau invented a way that divers could carry compressed air, in tanks on their backs. The system is known as SCUBA: Self-Contained Underwater Breathing Apparatus.

twist it!

The deepest any scuba diver has been able to go is 1,044 feet.

The greatest undersea journey took place in 1960, when two explorers dived to 35,797 feet in a submersible called the *Trieste*. It took them about five hours to reach the bottom of the Mariana Trench in the Pacific Ocean.

Robotic submersibles can explore the deep without putting any humans in danger. They are called Remotely Operated Vehicles, or ROVs for short.

The first diving suits were used in the 1830s. They were made of watertight rubber and canvas. Air was pumped from a boat above, through long tubes that were connected to the diver's metal helmet.

DEEP THOUGHTS

Musician Katie Melua has played at nearly 1,000 feet below sea level with a band, on a platform oil rig in the North Sea.

SUPERSUB!

Are you looking for an all-round vehicle with an extra thrill factor? Try the Dolphin and Seabreacher subs designed by Innespace of the USA. The fully enclosed vehicles can dive, jump, and roll, and travel up to 40 mph on the surface and 20 mph underwater.

People first went to explore the ocean depths just 200 years ago. They mostly went in search of valuable cargo, such as gold, which had sunk with shipwrecks.

Diving can be a deadly pastime. If divers return to the surface too quickly, the change in water pressure can give them the bends, a potentially fatal condition.

Ripley's Believe It or Not!®

Man's breath friend

Shadow is a scuba-diving dog that enjoys exploring underwater. He accompanies his owner, Dwane Folsom of the US, on scuba trips. Shadow wears his own special helmet and diving suit, and shares a breathing tube with Dwane.

Room with a view

If you're feeling rich and want to splash out on a hotel with a difference, check in at the Poseidon Underwater Hotel. Rooms will cost about $30,000 a week, but all guests get their own personal submarine to explore the underwater resort, plus a luxury room that sits 40 feet underwater, on the floor of a lagoon, with a view of the surrounding Fijian ocean life swimming by.

UP ANCHOR!

Traveling across oceans sometimes requires great courage to combat the combined forces of wind, waves, currents, and the planet's fiercest weather.

Long ago, mariners sailed or rowed across the oceans in search of new lands and opportunities. They found their way by following the stars, but many of them lost their lives in storms and shipwrecks. Most modern journeys make use of the latest technology, including boats that are equipped with communication and satellite navigation systems. Some ocean journeys are even made in the lap of luxury, such as on the *Oasis of the Seas*!

The ship is 1,187 feet long and 208 feet wide.

FUN FEATURES

- Water and light show with 65-feet high fountains
- A zipwire stretched between nine decks
- An ice rink
- Diving platforms and a trapeze
- Carousels and funfair activities

It has 2,706 guest rooms, 16 decks, 24 elevators, and nearly 2,000 balconies.

SEA MONSTER

The world's largest passenger ship has been described as a holiday village in the ocean—but with 8,000 people on board it's more like a town! The *Oasis of the Seas* is so big it even has room for tropical gardens with 56 growing trees, a science lab, and basketball courts.

AQUALANDS

CENTRAL PARK

Guests on the Oasis enjoy the chilling effects of 110,231 pounds of ice cubes every day.

ROYAL PROMENADE

CAROUSEL

BIG
WORD ALERT

CIRCUMNAVIGATION
A circumnavigation is a journey all the way around something. It usually refers to a sea voyage all the way around the world.

Twist it!

A motor yacht named *Dubai* was built for one of the world's richest men. It is so large there's room for a helicopter pad, cinema, gym, and squash court. It even has its own submarine!

When Ellen MacArthur broke the record for the fastest solo circumnavigation of the globe in 2005, she showed true powers of endurance. The feat took Ellen 71 days and 14 hours, and during that time she never slept for longer than 20 minutes at a time.

SEAFARERS

The first people to row across the Atlantic Ocean were George Harbo and Frank Samuelson of Norway. It took them nearly two months to row 3,270 miles in 1896.

TREASURE TROVE

The oceans and seas cover most of the Earth's surface. They are home to billions of living things, and contribute to the planet's health in many different ways. People have been relying on the oceans' rich produce for thousands of years.

Oceans provide food for billions of people around the world, as well as jobs for the people who catch fish. Long ago, people fished for just the food they needed, but now too many fish are being taken from the sea. Too little is being done to protect marine habitats, and too much garbage is being thrown into the oceans. There is some good news though, people all over the world are working hard to save our seas and create special places where ocean wildlife is safe.

SEAFOOD SHORTAGE

Tuna is one of the world's favorite fish to eat. In recent years, 95 percent of all bluefin tuna have been removed from the sea, and they could disappear completely soon.

Nearly half of all known types of animals and plants live in oceans.

FOOD FOR THOUGHT

The Inuit people of the Arctic enjoy a type of walrus meat called *igunaaq*. It is stored under a pile of stones and, over the course of one year, it freezes and thaws so many times it becomes a rotting, stinking mass. Yum!

Most countries of the world have agreed not to hunt whales for meat any more, but seven species of great whales are still in danger of dying out forever.

Ermis and Androniki Nicholas love fish and chips so much they travel 60 miles every day to the coast for a fish lunch; and they have been making this trip for ten years!

A high-energy drink on sale in Japan is made from... eels! It's yellow, fizzy, and still has the fish heads and bones in it.

twist it!

Pretty wasteful

Pieces of coral, seashells, and sea creatures are used to make souvenirs and sold to tourists all over the world. Pearls and sponges are also harvested from the sea. Many animals are killed and their habitats destroyed for this trade.

ANTARCTIC ANTIFREEZE

Fish that live in the icy Antarctic are able to survive thanks to special antifreeze chemicals in their bodies. They work by locking up ice crystals, to stop them from spreading. Scientists hope to copy the chemicals and make antifreeze paint for aircraft wings.

Doctors are using zebrafish and horseshoe crabs in an attempt to discover new medicines and repair damaged human hearts.

Some wind farms are located offshore so they can get maximum benefit from the strong gales that blow over the surface of the oceans.

JELLYFISH NOODLES

Scientists believe that the best way to make sure we don't use up all of the fish in the sea for food is to create marine reserves—areas in the oceans where no one is allowed to fish. Then, the endangered fish would be able to breed in these areas and increase their numbers once more. If we don't do this, some people believe that the only creatures left in the sea in large numbers for us to eat will be jellyfish! Jellyfish noodles, anyone?

RICH RESOURCES

The world's oceans provide a great deal of the energy we use in our everyday lives. Offshore platforms extract oil and natural gas from beneath the seabed, but one day these fuels, which are used to make power, will run out. New technology can harness the power of the wind and the waves to make electricity. These wind and wave farms provide a renewable, or never-ending, source of power that could give the world some of its energy in the future. Phew!

OCEANS INDEX

Bold numbers refer to main entries; numbers in *italic* refer to the illustrations

A

Abyss **30–31**, **40–41**
African penguins 24, *24*
aircraft 38, *38*, 44
albatrosses 25, *25*
algae 17, 20
amphibians 18
anchovies 18
angel fish 18, *18*
anglerfish 31, *31*
Antarctic 16, 44
antifreeze 44
archer fish 11, *11*
Arctic 45
armor **12–13**
Atlantic giant squid 16, *16*
Atlantic Ocean 43
atmosphere 6
Australia 15

B

babies
   blue whales 17, *17*
   cetaceans 26
backbones 18
bacteria 29, 30
"baitballs" 18, *18*
barnacles 39, *39*
barracudas 20, *20*
beaked sea snakes 35, *35*
beluga whales 27
Bermuda Triangle 38
big animals **16–17**
biodiversity **20–21**
bioluminescence 30
birds 18, **24–25**
blobfish 21, *21*
bloops 39
blue-footed boobies 24, *24*
blue penguins 24, *24*
blue whales 4, 17, *17*, 27
bluefin tuna fish 44, *44*
boats **42–43**
bombs 9
bones 23
boobies, blue-footed 24, *24*
boot-lace worms 17, *17*
boxer crabs 33, *33*
brain coral 5, *14*
breathing
   fish 18, 19
   mammals 26
bull sharks 23
butterfly fish, masked 18, *18*

C

calcium 12
camouflage 29
   cuttlefish 33

harlequin shrimps 28, *28*
octopuses 4
sargassum fish 33
sea snakes 35
sharks 22
candy flatworms 29, *29*
carapaces 12
carbon dioxide 9
cartilage 23
Cetaceans 26, 27
cilia 31, *31*
circumnavigation 43
clams 12
   giant clams 17, *17*
   razor clams 13
Clasen, Craig 23, *23*
climate 6
clouds 6, 7, *7*
clownfish 19, *19*
coastal areas **10–11**, 14
cockatoo squid *30–31*, 31
coconuts 12, *12–13*, 37
colonies
   coral reefs 5, 14–15
   Portuguese man o'war 35, *35*
colors **28–29**, 33, 34–35
colossal squid 16, 31
Columbus, Christopher 38
comb jellies 31, *31*
condensation, water cycle 7
continental shelf 11, *11*
copper 9
coral reefs 5, *5*, **14–15**, 45
Coral Triangle 5, 15
Cousteau, Jacques 40
cowries 12
crabs 12
   boxer crabs 33, *33*
   hermit crabs 13, *13*
   horseshoe crabs 44
   spider crabs 12, *12*
   strawberry crabs 28, *28*
crocodiles 11, 33
crustaceans 12, 33
cryptozoologists 38
currents 6, 9, 17, 36
cuttlefish 33
cyclones, tropical 7
Cyclops, USS 38, *38*

D

Dark Zone 8, 36
deep-sea creatures **30–31**
deep-sea explorers **40–41**
defenses **12–13**, 32
density, seawater 36
digging, razor clams 13
diving
   deep-sea explorers **40–41**
   free diving 8, *8*
   sperm whales 31
dog, scuba-diving 41, *41*
dog whelks 12

Dolphin submarine 40, *40*
dolphins 26, 27, *27*
Douglas DC-3 aircraft 38, *38*
drag 37
dragon moray eels 29, *29*
Dubai (motor yacht) 43
dugongs 26, 38

E

Earth 6
ecosystems 5, 14
eels 19, 45
eggs, fish 19, 21
electricity 44
elephant seals 27, *27*
energy 17, 32, 36, 44
Equator 6
evaporation, water cycle 7
explorers, deep-sea **40–41**
eyes
   spookfish 30, *30*
   squid 16, *16*

F

fan coral 5, *15*
fault lines 9
feathers 24
finger coral 5, *14*
fish **18–19**, **20–21**
fish and chips 44
fishing 44
flatfish 21
flatworms 29, *29*
flippers 27
floating 17, 36
flying fish 21, *21*
Folsom, Dwane 41, *41*
food 32
food poisoning 20
free diving 8, *8*

G

garibaldis 21, *21*
gas, natural 44
gases 6, 9
gentoo penguins 25, *25*, 37
gharials 11, *11*
gills 19
gliding 21
global conveyor 9
globsters 39
gold 9
goose barnacles 39, *39*
gravity, tides 6
Great Barrier Reef 5, 15
"great swallower" fish 19, *19*
great white sharks 23, *23*
Griffin, Dr. J. 38
guillemots 24, *24*
gulls 24, *24*

H

habitats 10, 20

hagfish 31
hair, marine mammals 26, 27
halibut 21
Harbo, George 43
harlequin shrimps 28, *28*
harlequin sweetlips 18, *18*
Harris, Jim 39
hermit crabs 13, *13*
herring gulls 24, *24*
herrings 19
horseshoe crabs 44
hot water vents 31
hotel, underwater 41, *41*
humpback whales 27
hurricanes 7, *7*
hydrothermal vents 31

I

ice, antifreeze 45
icebergs 6
India 11
Indonesia 15
Inuit people 44

J

jawfish 21
jellyfish 22, 29, *29*, 45, *45*

K

kelp 10, 11
killer whales 32, *32–33*, 37
krakens 39, *39*
krill 12, 17, 23, 26

L

lampreys 20
lantern fish 37
lantern sharks 22
leafy seadragons 32, *32*
leatherback turtles 37
lifespan, orange roughies 19
light 29, 30
lionfish 35, *35*
lobsters 12
   size 5
   spiny lobsters 36, *36–37*
   wallet found in claws of 13
Longman's beaked whale 39

M

MacArthur, Ellen 43
mackerel 33
mako sharks 37
Malaysia 15
mammals 18, **26–27**
manatees 38
mandarin fish 28, *28*
maned seahorses 36, *36*
mangrove trees 11, *11*
marine 8
marine snow 9, 30
masked butterfly fish 18, *18*
Mauna Kea 9

mauve stingers 29, *29*
megamouth 22
mermaids 38, *38*
Mexico, Gulf of 44
migration 36, 37
mine hunting 9
minerals 9, 12
molecules 17
mollusks 12
monsters **38–39**
Moon 6, 30
moray eels 29, *29*
Mount Everest 9, 40
mountains 9
mussels 10, *10*, 12
mysteries **38–39**

N

National Crab Racing Association 13
Nicholas, Ermis and Androniki 45
North Sea 17
Nova Scotia, Canada 6
nudibranchs 34, *34*

O

Oasis of the Seas 42–43, *43*
octopuses
    camouflage 4
    day octopus 4, *4*
    sea monsters 39
    veined octopus 12, *12–13*
oil platforms 44
orange roughies 19
oxygen
    in atmosphere 6
    deep-sea explorers 40
    gills 19
    sperm whales 31
    in water 9
oysters 12

P

Pacific Ocean 7
palm trees 37
parrot fish 19, *19*
particles 17, 36, 37
pearls 45, *45*
pelicans 5, 25, *25*
penguins 24, *24–25*, 32, *32–33*, 37
Petronius oil platform 44
pigments 29
pineapple fish 19, *19*
plankton 11, 22, 36
plants 11
poisons 20, 21, 33, **34–35**
polar bears 26, *26*
polar regions 6
polyps, coral 5, 14, 15
porcupine fish 32, *32*
porpoises 26
Portuguese man o' war 35, *35*

Poseidon, HMS 39
Poseidon Underwater Hotel 41, *41*
prawns 12
predators **12–13**, 21, 26, 28, **32–33**, 34
prey 32
puffins 25, *25*

R

rain 6, 7, *7*
rays 23
razor clams 13
razorfish 33, *33*
red devils 39
red shrimps 30, *30*
reefs 5, *5*, **14–15**
reptiles 18
requiem sharks 23
rip currents 6
rivers 10
robots, digging 13
rowing 43

S

sailfish 18, 37, *37*
salt 9
saltwater crocodiles 33
Samuelson, Frank 43
sandtiger sharks 23
sardines 18
sargassum fish 33
scaly-foot snails 13
schools, fish 19
SCUBA diving 40, 41, *41*
sculpture, underwater 15, *15*
sea anemones 33, 34, *34*
sea lions 4, 9, *9*, 27, 37
sea monsters **38–39**
sea otters 10, *10*
sea slugs 34, *34*
sea snails 13, *13*
sea snakes 35, *35*
sea urchins 12, 13, *13*
sea worms 39
Seabreacher submarine 40, *40*
seadragons 32, *32*
seagrass 26
seahorses 5, 36, *36*
seals 26, 27, 32
seawater 9, 17, 36
seaweeds 11
sharks **22–23**
    bull shark 23
    camouflage 22
    dolphins and 27
    great white shark 23, *23*
    lantern shark 22
    mako shark 37
    requiem shark 23
    sandtiger shark 23
    size 4
    skin 22
    speed 37

thresher shark 4
tiger shark 22, 23, *23*
whale shark 22, *22*
shells 12, 13, 29, 45
ships **42–43**
shipwrecks 38, 41, 42
shoals, fish 19, 33
shrimps 12
    harlequin shrimps 28, *28*
    red shrimps 30, *30*
singing, whales 27
size, sea creatures 4–5, **16–17**
skates 23
skeletons 23, 26
skin
    pigments 29
    sharks 22
skuas 25, *25*
snails, scaly-foot 13
snake mackerel 19, *19*
southeast Asia 34
Southern Ocean 9
spawning 19
speed 37
sperm whales 31
spider crabs 12, *12*
spines 20, 34, 35
spiny lobsters 36, *36–37*
sponges 45
spookfish 20, 30, *30*
squid
    Atlantic giant squid 16, *16*
    cockatoo squid 30 31, *31*
    colossal squid 16, 31
    sea monsters 39
staghorn coral 5, *15*
star coral 5, *14*
starfish 12, 13, *13*
stonefish 34, *34*
storms 7, *7*, 42
strawberry crabs 28, *28*
streamlining 19
submarines 40, *40*
submersibles 30, 41, *41*
Sun 6
Sunlight Zone 8, **10–11**, 28, 36, 37
surfing 25, *25*
swamps, mangrove 11, *11*
sweetlips, harlequin 18, *18*
swell, waves 6
swim bladders 19
swimming 19, 21, 27, **36–37**

T

Taylor, Jason de Caires 15, *15*
tectonic plates 9, *9*
teeth
    lampreys 20, *20*
    sharks 22
    wolf fish 32, *32*
thresher sharks 4
tides 6, *6*, 10

tiger sharks 22, 23, *23*
titan triggerfish 21
tongues, blue whales 27
toxins **34–35**
trees, mangrove 11, *11*
triggerfish 21
tropical cyclones 7, *7*
Trubridge, William 8, *8*
trumpetfish 19, *19*
tsunamis 8, *8*
tube worms 31
tuna fish 21, 44, *44*
turtles 37
tusks 26, *26*
Twilight Zone 31, 36
typhoons 7, *7*

U

US Navy 9

V

veined octopuses 12, *12–13*
venom **34–35**
vents, hydrothermal 31
vertebrates 18
volcanoes 9
vomiting, great white sharks 23

W

wallet, long-lost 13
walruses 26, *26*, 45
water cycle 7, *7*
wave power 44
waves 6
weather **6–7**
Westlake, Paul 13
whale sharks 22, *22*
whales 26
    beluga whale 27
    blue whale 4, 17, *17*, 27
    food 11
    humpback whale 27
    hunting 45
    Longman's beaked whale 39
    singing 27
    size 4
    sperm whale 31
    tongues 27
whiskers 26
wind farms 45, *45*
winds 7
wolf fish 32, *32*
worms 17, *17*, 31, 39

Z

zebrafish 44

ACKNOWLEDGMENTS

COVER David Fleetham/Taxi/Getty Images, (b/r) Greenpeace/Rex Features

2 (t) © nata_rass – Fotolia.com, (b) © javarman – Fotolia.com; **3** (t) Jim Morgan jmorgan8@cfl.rr.com, (r) Robert Innes; **4** (c) David Fleetham/Taxi/Getty Images; **4–5** (b) © aleksander1 – Fotolia.com; **6** (t, t/r) © Stephen Rees – iStock.com; **6–7** © Ramon Purcell – iStock.com; **7** (t/r) NASA/GSFC, MODIS Rapid Response; **8** (t/l, t/c, t/r) NASA/GSFC, MODIS Rapid Response; **8–9** Igor Liberti www.apnea.ch; **9** (t/r, b/r, b) U.S. Navy Photo; **10** (l) © Paul Allen – Fotolia.com, (b/c) Suzi Eszterhas/Minden Pictures/FLPA, (b/cl) Matthias Breiter/Minden Pictures/FLPA, (b/cr) © Lynn M. Stone, (b/l) © Oceans Image/Photoshot, (c/l) © NHPA/Photoshot; **11** (b/r, t/r) © NHPA/Photoshot (sp) © Alberto Pomares – iStock.com; **12–13** (c) Constantinos Petrinos/Nature Picture Library/Rex Features; **13** (t/r) Jeff Rotman/Naturepl.com, (c/r) Jim Morgan jmorgan8@cfl.rr.com, (b/r) David Fleetham/Bluegreenpictures.com; **14** (c) © Oceans Image/Photoshot, (b/l) © Monty Chandler – Fotolia.com; **14–15** (dp) © John Anderson – iStock.com, (b) David Espin – Fotolia.com; **15** (t/r) © Piero Malaer – iStock.com, (c/r) © Richard Carey – Fotolia.com, (b/r) Barcroft Media via Getty Images; **16–17** (dp) Jim Edds/Science Photo Library; **17** (c) Marlin.ac.uk/stevetrewhella@hotmail.com, (c/r) © David Fleetham/Bluegreenpictures.com, (b/r) © a_elmo – Fotolia.com, (b) © Mark Carwardine/naturepl.com; **18** (t/l) © pipehorse – Fotolia.com, (t/c) Georgette Douwma/Science Photo Library, (t/r) © Richard Carey – Fotolia.com; **18–19** Doug Perrine/Bluegreenpictures.com; **19** (t/l) © Richard Carey – Fotolia.com, (t/c) © nata_rass – Fotolia.com, (t/r) Birgit Koch/Imagebroker/FLPA, (c) P. Bush/Barcroft Media Ltd (b/r) Tommy Schultz – Fotolia.com; **20** (b/l) ImageBroker/Imagebroker/FLPA; **20–21** Gary Meszaros/Science Photo Library; **21** (t/r) © Oceans Image/Photoshot, (c) Michael Nolan/Splashdowndirect/Rex Features, (b/r) Greenpeace/Rex Features; **22** © Reinhard Dirscherl/FLPA; **23** (c) Brandon Cole/Bluegreenimages.com, (b/l) D.J. Struntz/Barcroft Media Ltd; **24** (t/r) International Antartic Centre, (t/c) California Academy of Sciences, (b/l) © javarman – Fotolia.com, (b/c) © Sergey Korotkov – iStock.com, (b/r) © Eric Isselée – Fotolia.com; **25** (c) Andy Rouse/Rex Features, (r) Ingo Arndt/Minden Pictures/FLPA, (b/l) iStock.com, (b/c) © Paul Tessier – iStock.com, (b/r) © Iain Sarjeant – iStock.com; **26** (t, b/l) © NHPA/Photoshot; **27** (t) Barry Bland/Barcroft Media Ltd, (b/r) © Nancy Nehring – iStock.com; **28** (t/r) Dreamstime.com, (c) © idy – Fotolia.com, (b/l) Quirky China/Rex Features; **28–29** (dp) © Ferran Traite Soler – iStock.com; **29** (t) © Alan James/Naturepl.com, (c) © Francesca Rizzo – iStock.com, (b) David Fleetham/Bluegreenpictures.com; **30** (b/l, b/r) David Shale/Bluegreenpictures.com; **30–31** (t) © Frans Lanting/Corbis, (c) © NHPA/Photoshot; **31** (b/r) David Shale/Bluegreenpictures.com; **32** (t) © Oceans-Image/Photoshot, (l) © Scott McCabe – iStock.com, (c/l) © Florian Graner/Naturepl.com; **32–33** (b) Norbert Wu/Minden Pictures/FLPA; **33** (t/r) David B Fleetham/PhotoLibrary, (c) © Markus Koller – Fotolia.com; **34** (t) © Kerry Werry – iStock.com, (b/l) © Achim Prill – iStock.com, (b/r) © John Anderson – iStock.com; **34–35** (dp) pablo del rio sotelo – iStock.com; **35** (t, c/r) © NHPA/Photoshot, (b) © Jacob Wackerhausen – iStock.com; **36** (t) © NHPA/Photoshot, (b) © Doug Perrine/naturepl.com; **37** (t) © Doug Perrine/Bluegreenpictures.com, (b/r) © aleksander1 – Fotolia.com; **38** (b) Rex Features (r) United States Naval History and Heritage Command photograph; **38–39** (dp) © Kevin Russ – iStock.com; **39** (t/l) iStock.com, (t/r) Professor Paul Brain/Wenn.com, (c) Time & Life Pictures/Getty Images, (b) © Stefanie Leuker – Fotolia.com; **40** (t) Robert Innes; **40–41** (c) © Robert Nu/FLPA; **41** (t/r, c/r) Rex Features, (b) Palm Beach Post/Rex Features; **42–43** KPA/Zuma/Rex Features; **44** Wild Wonders of Europe/Zankl/Bluegreenpictures.com; **45** (t) Norbert Wu/Minden Pictures/FLPA, (t/r) © Sean Gladwell – Fotolia.com, (b) Photolibrary.com/photofactory, (b/r) © Francesca Rizzo – iStock.com, (r) Woodfall Wild Images/Photoshot

Key: t = top, b = bottom, c = center, l = left, r = right, sp = single page, dp = double page, bgd = background
All other photos are from Ripley Entertainment Inc. All artwork by Rocket Design (East Anglia) Ltd.

Every attempt has been made to acknowledge correctly and contact copyright holders and we apologize in advance for any unintentional errors or omissions, which will be corrected in future editions.

Ripley's— **EXTREME EARTH** Believe It or Not!®

RIPLEY
PUBLISHING

a Jim Pattison Company

TWISTS

Written by Clint Twist, Lisa Regan, Camilla de la Bedoyere

Consultant Barbara Taylor

RIPLEY
PUBLISHING

Publisher Anne Marshall

Editorial Director Rebecca Miles
Project Editor Lisa Regan
Editorial Assistant Charlotte Howell
Picture Researchers James Proud, Charlotte Howell
Proofreader Judy Barratt
Indexer Hilary Bird

Art Director Sam South
Senior Designer Michelle Cannatella
Design Rocket Design (East Anglia) Ltd
Reprographics Juice Creative Ltd

www.ripleybooks.com

CONTENTS

WHAT'S INSIDE YOUR BOOK? 4

OUR PLACE IN SPACE
LIFE ON EARTH 6

CRACKING UP
A LOOK INSIDE 8

SHOCKS AND SHAKES
EARTHQUAKES 10

ROOF OF THE WORLD
MIGHTY MOUNTAINS 12

VIOLENT ERUPTIONS 14
VOLCANOES

REAL HARD
ROCKS AND MINERALS 16

PAGE 23

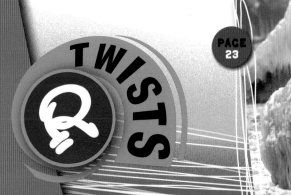

GOING UNDERGROUND
CAVES AND MINES
18

COMFORT BLANKET
THE ATMOSPHERE
20

UP IN THE AIR
WILD WEATHER
22

WATERWORLD
OCEAN COMMOTION
24

REMARKABLE REEFS
CORAL AND THE TROPICS
26

ON THE EDGE
COASTLINES
28

COOL WATERS
RIVERS, WATERFALLS, AND LAKES
30

RIVERS OF ICE
GROOVY GLACIERS
32

FROZEN WILDERNESS
POLAR REGIONS
34

DRY AS A BONE   DESERTS
36

PASTURES NEW
GRASSLANDS
38

WILD WOODLANDS
CONIFEROUS AND TEMPERATE FORESTS
40

STEAMY SURROUNDINGS
TROPICAL RAINFORESTS
42

EARTH IN DANGER
TIME IS RUNNING OUT
44

INDEX
46

PAGE
43

PAGE
29

WHAT ON EARTH!
OUR HOME

Welcome to your world! It's easy to spend your time on this planet, making the most of its rich resources, without stopping to think about what the Earth is really like. It's home to over six billion people, and provides all we need: food, water, shelter, energy, and even the air that we breathe is safe because of Earth's atmosphere.

Take a look around and you'll see amazing features of breathtaking beauty. Earth is the only planet in our Solar System to have our spectacular combination of mountains, oceans, volcanoes, deserts, and rainforests. So read on and prepare to be amazed at our world.

Do the twist

This book is packed with superb sights created by nature. It will teach you amazing things about our planet, but like all Twists books, it shines a spotlight on things that are unbelievable but true. Turn the pages and find out more...

Learn fab fast facts to go with the cool pictures.

HOT AND COLD

These Japanese macaques like it hot—even when it's cold. They keep warm in winter temperatures of 5°F by bathing in natural hot springs. Macaque babies also roll snowballs, just for fun!

TWISTS

EARTH EXTREMES...	Coldest Antarctica −129°F	Hottest El Azizia, Ethiopia 136°F	Windiest Antarctica 190 mph	Wettest (average) Mount Wai-'ale-'ale, Kauai, Hawaii, about 500 inches a year

Found a new word? Big word alerts will explain it for you.

Ripley explains some of the geographical know-how behind features on our planet.

Don't forget to look out for the "twist it!" column on some pages. Twist the book to find out more fast facts about the world we live in.

ROOF of the WORLD
MIGHTY MOUNTAINS

Majestic mountain ranges are nature's way of showing off! Their spectacular peaks are capped in clouds and mist and cloaked with snow and ice.

Mountains are created by the slow-moving forces that cause the Earth's plates to collide. Over time, rock is thrust upward, crumpling and folding into beautiful shapes. It takes millions of years, but as soon as mountains form, erosion and weathering start to wear them down. As ice freezes and thaws near the peaks, rocks split and break away, leaving sharp pyramid-like tops, while running water and glaciers produce softer, more rounded edges. Eventually, the mountains will be completely worn away!

SUMMIT A summit is the highest part of a mountain.

BIG WORD ALERT

Ripley explains...

Mountains are pushed upward

Continental crust — Continental crust

Plates move together

When two continental plates collide, the rocks on both plates become compressed (squashed) and folded. Over millions of years, the folds are forced higher and higher above the surrounding surface. Mountains are formed in this way.

New Zealand's highest peak is Mount Cook. In 1991 the top 33 feet fell off in an avalanche.

Mount Everest is known as Sagarmatha in Nepalese.

he world's second highest mountain
It is nearly 800 feet
r than Everest.

The tallest peaks are in the Himalayas in southern Asia. The world's highest mountain, Mount Everest in Nepal, is here and measures 29,035 feet. The Himalayas were formed when the Indian and Eurasian plates collided about 45 million years ago.

ummits are a collection of the ntains on each continent. The o climb all seven was Canadian 1986.

ca: Denali (20,320 feet)
ca: Aconcagua (22,830 feet)
us (18,510 feet)
anjaro (19,340 feet)
(29,035 feet)
Carstenz Pyramid (16,023 feet)
son Massif (16,067 feet)

There are two "base camps" on Everest, both at just over 17,000 feet. Climbers camp there on the way up and down the mountain, eating, resting, and acclimatizing (getting used to being so high up).

ICED DINNER
Seven people sat down to eat a live-course meal that they had prepared on a mountain in Tibet. They carried their food, plus table, chairs, silver cutlery, wine, flowers, and candles to a height of 22,000 feet, and even dressed the part with top hats and smart suits and ties.

Mountain memorial
A giant face in the rocky mountainside in South Dakota's Black Hills forms part of a memorial to the area's Native Americans. The sculpture was started in 1948 and still has lots of work to be done—eventually the mountain will have a whole figure riding a horse. It is being blasted out of the rock to honor Chief Crazy Horse.

563 FEET HIGH!

13

twist it!

pants, and an overcoat.
snow and slept barefoot wearing just a shirt.
as low as -20°F
Nepal, who trekked barefoot through the
1960s was followed by a pilgrim from
A US expedition to the Himalayas in the

vows there in May 2005.
highest peak. They exchanged their
the top of Mount Everest, the world's
were the first couple to get married at
Mona Mule Pati and Pem Dorjee Sherpa

lowest point in the USA.
Zabriskie Point in Death Valley—the
California. It is less than 80 miles from
(outside Alaska) is Mount Whitney,
The highest mountain in the USA

as plates moved apart.
became separated by the Atlantic Ocean
Mountains in North America, until they
were once part of the Appalachian
The Caledonian Mountains of Scotland

HIGH HOPES

Ripley's Believe It or Not!

RARE ROCK
A stone covered with long white "hair" is so rare it has been valued at over a million dollars. The hair is strands of fossilized fungus formed over millions of years.

Twists are all about Believe It or Not: amazing facts, feats, and things that will make you go "Wow!".

Look for the Ripley R to find out even more than you knew before!

Driest
Atacama Desert, Chile, no rain since records began

Tallest
Mount Everest
29,035 feet

Deepest
Pacific Ocean (Mariana Trench) 35,837 feet

Iciest
Antarctica has 90 percent of Earth's ice

OUR PLACE IN SPACE

Welcome to planet Earth, a spinning ball of hot rock that flies through space at more than 67,000 miles an hour. The world is our home and we love it! Earth is one of eight planets that circles the Sun, and the Sun is just one of billions of stars in our galaxy—the Milky Way. What makes Earth so special? So far, it's the only place in the entire Universe we know of where life exists.

Feeling dizzy? You should be, because you're not only flying around the Sun, you're also spinning at 1,000 miles an hour as the Earth turns. It's the way the Earth spins on its own axis, and orbits the Sun, that gives us measurements of time, including our 24-hour days, our 365-day years and our seasons.

SUN

It takes eight minutes for light from the Sun to reach the Earth. It is the Sun's light and heat, and the fact that Earth has water and a safe atmosphere, that allows life on Earth.

YOU ARE HERE

Earth facts

- Diameter: 7,928 miles
- Circumference: 25,000 miles
- Surface area: 200 million square miles
- Estimated mass: 5,976 billion billion tons
- Distance from Sun: 93 million miles

Ripley's Believe It or Not!®

OLD MAN

Human ancestors have been on Earth for millions of years. Scientists think that people similar to us developed around 250,000 years ago. This 5,000-year-old ice-preserved body helps scientists learn about people from the past.

Loving life

Living things are grouped into five kingdoms. The smallest unit in these kingdoms is the species, which consists of all the organisms that share the same characteristics. All species have a Latin name. The name of our own species is *Homo sapiens* (which means "wise man"). Which kingdom do you think we fit into?

ANIMALS
- Can move around
- Cannot make their own food
- Have more than one cell

PLANTS
- Are usually green
- Can make their own food
- Have more than one cell

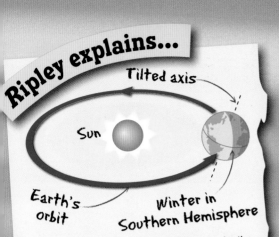

Ripley explains...

Tilted axis

Sun

Earth's orbit

Winter in Southern Hemisphere

The Earth is tilted in relation to the Sun. As the Earth makes its 365-day journey around the Sun, different parts of it are tilted toward, or away from, the Sun's light and heat. The Sun's light and heat hit the different places on Earth at different angles, giving some places more sunlight in summer and less in winter.

SUPER PLANET

The largest animal species that has ever lived is alive today. A full-grown blue whale can reach 100 feet in length and weigh 150 tons.

Scientists estimate there are about 20 million different living species on Earth, of which only about 10 percent have been identified and described.

A mushroom fossil found in Myanmar, Asia, is thought to be as much as 100 million years old.

The Earth is slowing down! It is spinning on its axis less quickly, and scientists say it may be significant enough for days in the future to have 25 hours instead of 24.

Fossils of sea creatures have been found near the top of Mount Everest.

twist it!

BIG WORD ALERT

AXIS
Imaginary line drawn through the center of the Earth from the North Pole to the South Pole.

Fossil finds

Fossils are living things that have been turned to rock over millions of years. They provide evidence of creatures that lived long ago, and allow scientists to work out what has been happening with life on our planet.

FUNGI

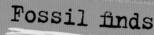

- Cannot make their own food
- Produce spores, not seeds e.g. yeast, mould
- Have more than one cell

PROTISTA

- Have only one cell
- Often live in soil or water e.g. amoeba

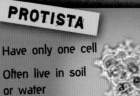

MONERA

- Have only one cell
- Very simple e.g. bacteria

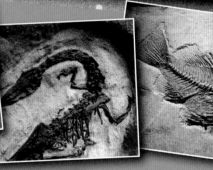

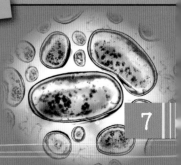

CRACKING UP
A LOOK INSIDE

There are 14 large plates and 38 smaller plates. Seven of the larger plates roughly match up to the continents of the world.

The plates carrying North America and Europe are moving away from one another at a speed of about 6 feet every 75 years. That means the two continents are getting farther away from each other at about the same rate your fingernails are growing!

The world is cracking up! The planet's outermost layer is a thick band of rock, called the crust—and it's in pieces. These pieces, known as plates, fit together like a giant jigsaw puzzle.

Strangely, plates are always on the move, stretching and squashing into one another as their edges grow or get sucked down into a super-hot layer of molten rock below. This whole fantastical process is called plate tectonics, and these crusty clashes are to blame for volcanoes, rift valleys, mountains, and earthquakes.

About 250 million years ago, all of today's landmasses were joined in one super-continent called Pangaea. As the Earth's plates moved, at maximum speeds of just 4¾ inches a year, it was pulled apart.

Mantle

Crust

Inner core

Outer core

The Earth has three layers: the crust, the mantle, and the core. The mantle is a thick layer of molten (liquid) rock with temperatures up to 5,800°F. Below is Earth's core where temperatures rise above 9,000°F. The outer core is liquid, but the pressure keeps the inner core solid.

The supercontinent of Pangaea was surrounded by a single ocean called Panthalassa. Look carefully at this map and you might see some familiar continent shapes.

Hot stuff

It's your fault

Some of the world's worst earthquakes happen along fault lines. The San Andreas Fault in California marks the boundary between the Pacific and North American plates. The fault line extends at least 10 miles into the Earth, and stretches for over 700 miles from north to south.

AROUND THE WORLD

The interior of the Earth is kept hot by heat from when the planet first formed, heat produced by radioactive elements, and heat from small dense particles colliding as they sink toward the center of the Earth.

Although the Earth's crust is made of rock and is solid, it is actually nearly 50 percent oxygen.

The South Pacific island of Niuatoputapu is the fastest-moving place on Earth, moving at 10 inches a year.

Margaret Hegarty of Concord, North Carolina, is the oldest woman to run a marathon on each of the seven continents. She was 76 when she completed the task, but has carried on running well into her 80s.

twist it!

Lava lover

Volcanic craters are a kind of window to the inner Earth. The hot, molten rock (called magma) in the mantle can push its way to the surface, where it comes out as lava.

Patrick Koster from the Netherlands has spent ten years photographing volcanoes and loves them so much that he proposed to his wife at the edge of a crater. He even reorganized his honeymoon so that he didn't miss a major eruption.

SHOCKS AND SHAKES

EARTH'S POWER

Hold on tight—the Earth's moving! For a few terrifying seconds the ground shakes and quakes. Buildings topple and great cracks appear in the Earth's surface as it rips open—this is the awesome power of an earthquake.

These mighty Earth movements happen in an instant, but they build up over a long time. As the Earth's plates grind against one another they build up tension. One sudden slip is all it takes for all that stored energy to be released, with ferocious force. Entire cities may be destroyed in an earthquake, bringing misery, chaos, and death.

Japan has many Earth tremors every year. Most of them are too small to cause much damage. However, in 1995, a massive earthquake hit the area around the city of Kobe. Nearly 7,000 people died and over 45,000 homes were ruined. The collapsed during the quake, which only raised section of the Hanshin motorway lasted for about 20 seconds.

Read all about it

The exact location of an earthquake is known as the epicenter. Scientists use sensitive instruments known as seismographs to measure the energy waves from an earthquake. By combining readings from seismographs around the world, they can work out the position of the epicenter.

The epicenter of the Kobe quake was miles below the Earth's surface.

It cost over $1 billion to repair and rebuild the city.

Many "aftershocks" caused more damage after the main quake.

QUAKE UPDATE:

April 30, 1906

The fires in San Francisco burned for three days. Over a quarter of a million people were made homeless, and at least 3,000 people were killed. Nearly 500 city blocks—at least 25,000 buildings—were destroyed.

ALL SHOOK UP

The island of Ranongga in the South Pacific was lifted out of the water by 10 feet in 2007, by an earthquake that measured 8.1 on the Richter scale.

An earthquake in Mexico in 1985 was strong enough to shake water out of a swimming pool 1,240 miles away in Tucson, Arizona.

Hundreds of hibernating snakes came out from their underground hideaways in China, just before an earthquake struck in 1975.

A 2007 earthquake was powerful enough to throw back a torpedo boat that had sunk in World War II.

The shock waves forming an earthquake can travel between 3¾ miles a second and 6¾ miles a second, depending whether they are in the Earth's core or near the surface.

Clever creatures

Japanese scientists believe the deep-sea oarfish, which usually lives at depths of more than 650 feet, helps them to predict earthquakes by appearing at the surface before tremors are felt.

>>Double disaster<<

The mountainous province of Sichuan in southwest China was hit by an earthquake in May, 2008. Nearly 90,000 people were either killed or reported missing. A year later, a landslide destroyed this bridge—part of a main road used while trying to rebuild the devastated area—killing even more people.

April 18, 1906

DISASTER STRIKES SAN FRANCISCO

An earthquake lasting only a minute struck San Francisco at 5:12 this morning, and has caused the worst damage seen in this nation's history. Fires are raging through the city, leaving people without homes, work, belongings, and loved ones.

Eyewitnesses report seeing buildings crushed like a biscuit in your hand, the ground moving in waves like the ocean, and the earth slipping from beneath their feet. Some streets have sunk by 4 feet; others have been pushed up to form 5-foot-high waves of rubble.

One result of earthquakes is that the shaking can cause some soils to behave like liquids, so that buildings sink into the ground.

ROOF of the WORLD

MIGHTY MOUNTAINS

Majestic mountain ranges are nature's way of showing off! Their spectacular peaks are capped in clouds and mist and cloaked with snow and ice.

Mountains are created by the slow-moving forces that cause the Earth's plates to collide. Over time, rock is thrust upward, crumpling and folding into beautiful shapes. It takes millions of years, but as soon as mountains form, erosion and weathering start to wear them down. As ice freezes and thaws near the peaks, rocks split and break away, leaving sharp pyramid-like tops, while running water and glaciers produce softer, more rounded edges. Eventually, the mountains will be completely worn away!

New Zealand's highest peak is Mount Cook. In 1991 the top 33 feet fell off in an avalanche.

Mount Everest is known as Sagarmatha in Nepalese.

K2 is the world's second highest mountain. It is nearly 800 feet shorter than Everest.

The tallest peaks are in the Himalayas in southern Asia. The world's highest mountain, Mount Everest in Nepal, is here and measures 29,035 feet. The Himalayas were formed when the Indian and Eurasian plates collided about 45 million years ago.

The Seven Summits are a collection of the highest mountains on each continent. The first person to climb all seven was Canadian Pat Morrow in 1986.

There are two "base camps" on Everest, both at just over 17,000 feet. Climbers camp there on the way up and down the mountain, eating, resting, and acclimatizing (getting used to being so high up).

- North America: Denali (20,320 feet)
- South America: Aconcagua (22,830 feet)
- Europe: Elbrus (18,510 feet)
- Africa: Kilimanjaro (19,340 feet)
- Asia: Everest (29,035 feet)
- Australasia: Carstenz Pyramid (16,023 feet)
- Antarctic: Vinson Massif (16,067 feet)

Ripley explains...

Mountains are pushed upward

Continental crust

Continental crust

Plates move together

When two continental plates collide, the rocks on both plates become compressed (squashed) and folded. Over millions of years, the folds are forced higher and higher above the surrounding surface. Mountains are formed in this way.

A US expedition to the Himalayas in the 1960s was followed by a pilgrim from Nepal, who trekked barefoot through the snow and slept outdoors in temperatures as low as −20°F wearing just a shirt, pants, and an overcoat.

Mona Mule Pati and Pem Dorjee Sherpa were the first couple to get married at the top of Mount Everest, the world's highest peak. They exchanged their vows there in May 2005.

The highest mountain in the USA (outside Alaska) is Mount Whitney, California. It is less than 80 miles from Zabriskie Point in Death Valley—the lowest point in the USA.

The Caledonian Mountains of Scotland were once part of the Appalachian Mountains in North America, until they became separated by the Atlantic Ocean as plates moved apart.

HIGH HOPES

Mountain memorial

A giant face in the rocky mountainside in South Dakota's Black Hills forms part of a memorial to the area's Native Americans. The sculpture was started in 1948 and still has lots of work to be done—eventually the mountain will have a whole figure riding a horse. It is being blasted out of the rock to honor Chief Crazy Horse.

563 FEET HIGH!

FASCINATING FACT! FASCINATING FACT! FASCINATING FACT!

ICED DINNER

Seven people sat down to eat a five-course meal that they had prepared on a mountain in Tibet. They carried their food, plus table, chairs, silver cutlery, wine, flowers, and candles to a height of 22,000 feet, and even dressed the part with top hats and smart suits and ties.

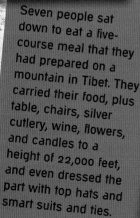

VIOLENT ERUPTIONS

VOLCANOES

When a mountain comes to life, and starts spouting smoke and spewing lava, it's clearly no ordinary mountain. Mighty volcanoes sit on top of the Earth's hot spots.

Super-heated rock bubbles quietly beneath the surface until its energy can no longer be contained—and an explosive force erupts. Boiling liquid rock, poisonous gases, ash, and volcanic bombs all spew out of active volcanoes, spelling tragedy and devastation for people living nearby. When volcanoes are quiet, between eruptions, they are described as dormant, and when they are no longer active at all, volcanoes are said to be extinct.

The temperature of lava inside a crater can reach 2,700°F, that's nearly one third the temperature of the Sun's surface.

The 1883 eruption of Krakatoa created a tsunami that was 130 feet high.

The Indonesian volcano Krakatoa killed over 36,000 people when it erupted in 1883. 165 towns and villages were destroyed and another 132 were badly damaged. Debris was blown 22 miles into the sky, and the noise of the eruption could be heard over 4,500 miles away in Sri Lanka. In 2009, the volcano began erupting again.

Bubbling under

The mud-filled crater of Totumo volcano in Colombia is a popular bathing spot! The hot mud is supposed to have beneficial effects on the human body.

IN HOT WATER

Extreme surfer CJ Kanuha surfed within 20 feet of the lava flow from Kilauea volcano on Hawaii's Big Island. The molten rock heats the sea to 400°F and it melted the wax on his surfboard.

The world's tallest volcano is Ojos del Salado in the South American Andes. It towers 22,608 feet above sea level, on the Chile–Argentina border.

Volcanic stones, known as pumice stones, are full of trapped air so weigh much less than you would expect. It's possible to lift a pumice stone twice your own size.

The volcano rabbit is found only on the slopes of four volcanoes near Mexico City, Mexico.

Some 60 percent of the population of Central America lives within 25 miles of an active or dormant volcano.

The world's largest volcano is Mauna Loa (height 13,681 feet), which occupies about half the island of Hawaii.

READY STEADY BLOW!

Ripley explains...

The plates that form the Earth's top layer can move away from each other, allowing the molten rock beneath to push its way to the Earth's surface.

Crater

Cloud of steam, ash, and gas

Cone-shaped peak

Lava flow

Magma chamber

Buried in ash

In 79 AD Mount Vesuvius erupted and buried the Roman town of Pompeii under 20 feet of ash. Archeologists discovered casts of the bodies of some of the unfortunate inhabitants who were buried as they tried to hide or escape.

Blown sky high

This photograph is of Sarychev Peak, next door to Russia and Japan. It erupted in 2009, blowing a 5-mile tower of smoke, ash, and steam into the air and through a hole blown in the clouds by the force. The picture was taken from the International Space Station, orbiting the Earth.

BIG WORD ALERT

MAGMA
The molten rock from deep inside the Earth. It is called lava once it has made its way to the surface.

REAL HARD

ROCKS AND MINERALS

Think rocks are dull? Think again, because some of them are shiny or colorful, and a few even contain precious minerals and gems, such as diamonds! There are three main types of rock: igneous, metamorphic, and sedimentary.

The type of rock that forms in the Earth's crust depends on three things: temperature, pressure, and the recipe of minerals it contains. When these three factors play their part, a soup of minerals can be transformed into different rocks, such as a smooth, sparkling white marble, or a salt-and-pepper patterned granite. And if rocks get very hot and squashed again, they melt back into a mineral magma soup!

FIRE ROCKS

Igneous rocks form from magma that has cooled and turned hard when it came close to, or burst through, the Earth's surface. The Giant's Causeway on the coast of Northern Ireland is made up of about 40,000 columns of the igneous rock basalt that were pushed up millions of years ago.

SET IN STONE

Sedimentary rocks are formed from sediments, such as sand and clay, that are deposited by wind and water. These amazing sandstone stripes are part of the Coyote Buttes and are known as The Wave. They were formed around 190 million years ago on the border of Arizona and Utah, USA. Over time, the sandstone has been eroded into the fascinating swirling shapes.

Rock formation

These may look just like piles of stones—very cleverly balanced, you must admit—but they're more than that. They are "inukshuk," stone landmarks built by many Arctic people. Enukso Point on Baffin Island, Canada, is a national historic site containing over 100 of these stone structures.

Igneous rocks are sometimes called fire rocks because they were formed from volcanic material.

ROCK 'N' ROLL

Certain types of the sedimentary rock limestone are composed entirely of the compressed shells of prehistoric sea creatures.

In 1906, a miner named Lindsay Hicks was buried inside Granite Mountain, California, after a mine cave-in. He was covered by thousands of tons of rock, but was rescued unharmed after 15 days.

Rocks have been forming and changing for millions of years. If you climb the Guadalupe Mountains in Texas you will be touching limestone that was once a tropical reef, about 250 million years ago.

twist it!

BIG WORD ALERT

GEOLOGISTS
Scientists who study rocks.

RARE ROCK

A stone covered with long white "hair" is so rare it has been valued at over a million dollars. The hair is strands of fossilized fungus formed over millions of years.

ALL CHANGE

Metamorphic rocks are rocks that have been metamorphosed (changed into something else) by volcanic heat and pressure. Slate, for example, is metamorphosed shale, and limestone turns into marble. Many of the world's mountain ranges contain metamorphic rocks. These rocks in the Swiss Alps have been changed further by glacier movement smoothing and scratching them.

GOING UNDERGROUND
CAVES AND MINES

Hidden from view, below the ground, are some of the Earth's most amazing natural wonders. Enormous caves and labyrinths of tunnels weave between solid rocks, carved out by the powerful force of water.

Rainwater and river water can seep through the cracks in rocks to form underground rivers. Water also dissolves some rocks, such as limestone, turning it into a liquid that drips and hardens again, to create amazing stalactites and stalagmites.

Some tunnels and caves owe more to people power. Valuable minerals such as coal form deep underground, and miners remove them by cutting into the rock, creating tunnels and caves.

The crystals are made of gypsum and are translucent.

The biggest crystals are 39 feet long.

CRYSTAL CAVE

These crystal daggers are as long as a bus! They were found by miners in 2000, around a thousand feet below the ground. They are part of the Naica Mine in Mexico, which has other caves containing smaller—but still spectacular—crystal formations.

Miners had to pump water out of the cave to clear it.

18

Light up, light up

Cave tours in New Zealand let you see in the dark! The roof of this cave is covered with glowing fireflies. The creatures are actually beetles and can flash their lights to attract other fireflies. They make the light on their abdomen by allowing air to mix with a special substance they produce.

The world's longest system of underground caves is the Mammoth Cave complex below Kentucky, USA, which extends over 352 miles—about the distance from Los Angeles to San Francisco—and has a maximum depth of 377 feet.

Temperatures in Coober Pedy, in the Australian outback, reach an uncomfortable 120°F, and so the people there have moved somewhere cooler: underground. There are a range of houses to choose from, plus museums, shops, churches, and hotels.

COOL DOWN

DEEP THOUGHTS

The deepest oil well ever drilled is the Tiber well that goes 35,055 feet below the seabed in the Gulf of Mexico. This means that the bottom of the well is more than 39,000 feet below sea level, and deeper than Mount Everest is high.

Blackwater rafting is a thrill-a-minute sport that takes participants through the caves of New Zealand—on an inner tube! Underground rivers carry along the tubes through dark passages that can be full of eels.

Starting in 1906, William Schmidt spent 38 years digging an underground passage through the El Paso Mountains of California. He burrowed for 2,087 feet and through 2,600 tons of rock.

twist it!

BIG WORD ALERT

SPELEOLOGY
The science of exploring underground spaces.

COMFORT BLANKET

THE ATMOSPHERE

The atmosphere around our planet keeps it nice and cosy! This thick layer of air is a rich mix of gases that protects us from the burning rays of the Sun, and keeps the heat in at night, like a comforting blanket.

That's not all we have to thank the atmosphere for: one of its top jobs is creating climate. The bottom layer of the atmosphere is called the troposphere and this is where weather happens. Liquid water spends part of its time as water vapor, high in the sky, and some of the water that falls today as rain was once drunk by dinosaurs!

The auroras are sometimes called the Northern Lights or Southern Lights.

SKY LIGHTS

Amazing light displays appear in the highest layers of the atmosphere and can be seen near the North and South poles. They are called the aurora borealis (say or-ora bor-ee-ar-lis) in the north and aurora australis (say or-ora os-trar-lis) in the south. The lights are created by a reaction between atoms from the Sun and gases in the Earth's atmosphere.

Sometimes the lights move and dance or shimmer.

Ripley's Believe It or Not!

All hail

Hailstones can grow really big—like these ones found after a hailstorm in Kansas in 1999.

HEAD IN THE CLOUDS

Clouds form different shapes at different heights, and depending how much water or ice they contain. Thin, wispy clouds high in the sky are known as cirrus clouds. This one, seen over Wellington in New Zealand, has been blown into the shape of a deer!

Ripley explains...

Rain falls from clouds

Condenses into cloud

Water evaporates

Rainwater flows to the sea

Water in the oceans—or even in a puddle—evaporates (turns to gas) and mixes with the air. It is carried by the wind until it condenses (turns back to water), making clouds. It falls back to the ground as precipitation and the cycle starts all over again.

twist it!

Up to 100 tons of space dust falls into the Earth's atmosphere every day. That's about the same weight as 20 African elephants.

NASA satellites have shown that the two sunniest places in the world are patches in the Pacific Ocean, south of Hawaii, and in the Sahara Desert in Niger.

Mount Waialeale, on Kauai in Hawaii, has rain nearly every day of the year. Only a few miles away on the coast, they get as little rain as 20 inches in a whole year.

RAIN OR SHINE

Within the troposphere, the air temperature drops by about 3.6°F per 1,000 feet of altitude.

This house was damaged by a tornado—it had one end blown off completely, but the inside was left intact. The dishes in the pantry weren't even broken!

FASCINATING FACT! FASCINATING FACT! FASCINATING FACT!

BIG WORD ALERT

PRECIPITATION Any kind of wetness coming from the sky: rain, snow, sleet, hail, and even fog.

FUNNEL VISION

A tornado is a whirling funnel of air formed in some thunderstorms. They can travel at high speeds of 250 mph and cause chaos and destruction. They happen in many parts of the world, but are frequent and famous in the central states of the USA, which are known as "tornado alley."

BEND IT

A rainbow is formed by sunlight being refracted (bent) by raindrops. You will only see a rainbow if the sun is behind you.

UP IN THE AIR
WILD WEATHER

Take a look outside—is the weather looking wild or mild? Right this moment there are about 2,000 thunderstorms and 100 flashes of lightning zapping through the sky, all over the world. Just one flash of supercharged lightning contains enough energy to light 150 million light bulbs!

Extreme weather might get you off school, but it can play havoc with people's lives. In the globe's cold spots, temperatures dip below a supercool 5°F in winter, while coastal areas can be hit by storm surges, gale force winds, and heavy rains that bring cliffs crashing to the ground.

An average lightning storm can discharge sufficient power to supply the entire USA with electricity for 20 minutes.

In 1998, during a soccer game in the Democratic Republic of Congo, all 11 players on one team were killed by lightning. None of the other team was struck.

A single lightning strike in Utah, in 1918, killed 504 sheep in one blast.

Ray Cauldwell, a baseball pitcher for the Cleveland Indians, was struck by lightning while playing. He was knocked unconscious but came to and carried on playing—and was on the winning side!

Kenneth Libbrecht of California has found a way to take photos of snowflakes. The results are beautiful, and show the six-sided formation of each individual flake.

CRYSTAL CLEAR

If the air in the atmosphere is cold enough, the rising water vapor (see Ripley explains, page 21) freezes instead of turning to liquid. This forms six-sided crystals: snowflakes. The air near the ground needs to be below freezing, too, or the crystals will turn to rain as they fall.

FREAKY FREEZE

Residents near Lake Geneva were shocked by scenes in January 2005. Gale-force winds carried water droplets from the lake, which froze on anything in their path because of 10°F temperatures.

Really wild

A hurricane is the most awesomely powerful of all weather events. The largest hurricanes extend 600–1,000 miles in diameter and produce winds up to 200 mph. They are caused by rising warm air over the ocean. As the storm reaches land, it begins to die out— but can still last for days and cause devastating damage.

HOME ALONE

A hurricane raged across Texas in 2008 and completely flattened buildings and trees. The only house left standing in one area was that of Warren and Pam Adams. They had lost a previous home to a 2005 hurricane, so had wisely built their new one on 14-foot-high columns to withstand the storms.

SNOW DONUTS

These amazing snow rollers, or snow donuts, are formed naturally when a clump of soft snow falls into hard snow at the top of a slope. They are quite rare, but Mike Stanford found these ones in Washington State in 2007 that were big enough to poke his head through!

>> Fenced in <<

The 2008 hurricane in Texas left these fish high and dry! The storms caused huge floods, which carried these fish up to 4 feet high and left them stuck in the links of a fence.

WATERWORLD

We call our planet Earth, but a better name might be Water—because more than 70 percent of the world's surface is actually covered by oceans and seas.

The biggest and deepest ocean is the Pacific and it contains more than half of the entire planet's seawater. While lakes and rivers have fresh water, which we can drink, oceans and seas are salty. There are five main zones, or layers, in the oceans, from just below the surface to the darkest depths.

0–656 feet

656–3,280 feet

The menacing-looking fangtooth fish only grows to about 6 inches, but its teeth are the largest of any ocean fish compared to its body size.

The maximum depth humans can reach with scuba equipment is just less than 1,000 feet.

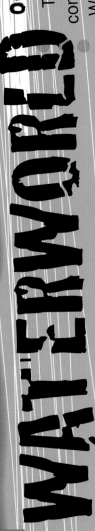

SUNLIGHT (EPIPELAGIC) ZONE

Jellyfish are found in all of the world's oceans. They have no heart, brain, or blood and use their tentacles to trap food.

The ferocious bull shark swims close to shore, so is a potential danger to humans taking a swim. They live in the warm waters of the ocean, but can also swim upriver and don't mind the fresh waters of the Amazon and Mississippi.

Free divers such as Herbert Nitsch from Austria, can dive to 700 feet with no breathing equipment except their lungs.

TWILIGHT (MESOPELAGIC) ZONE

twist it!

In 1990 ocean adventurer Tom McClean sailed across the Atlantic in a boat shaped like a bottle. Onboard he had a four poster bed!

From the top of Mount Irazu in Costa Rica you can see both the Pacific Ocean and the Atlantic Ocean.

Columbus landed in America in the 15th century.

The Atlantic Ocean is still growing at a rate of 1½ inches per year. This means it was about 66 feet narrower when Columbus landed in America in the 15th century.

Scientists have calculated that there are about the same number of molecules in a spoonful of water as there are spoonfuls of water in the Atlantic Ocean.

MAKING A SPLASH

24

MIDNIGHT (BATHYPELAGIC) ZONE

The sperm whale can dive deeper than most other whales—probably as deep as 8,200 feet. The water pressure is so great that it squashes its rib cage—but the whale's ribs are designed to fold up so they stay unhurt.

Giant squid are so big they can eat fish, crabs, and even sharks. They catch their prey by coiling up their tentacles around their victim. The squid must watch out, though—they are the chosen food of the sperm whale.

ABYSS (ABYSSOPELAGIC) ZONE

Manned submersibles such as the US Alvin dive to depths of around 15,000 feet to study ocean life.

TRENCH (HADALPELAGIC) ZONE

Hydrothermal vents appear at plate boundaries on the ocean floor. Water seeps into the Earth's crust and is heated by the magma, then shoots back up through cracks in the ocean floor.

The dumbo octopus gets its name from its ear-shaped fins that make it look like an elephant. It moves by flapping these fins to push itself through the water.

The unmanned robotic sub Nereus, developed by the Woods Hole Oceanographic Institution in the USA, is the only such vehicle that is capable of making the almost 7-mile journey to the deepest part of the trench.

25

REMARKABLE REEFS
CORAL AND THE TROPICS

Coral reefs can grow enormous, but they are built by tiny animals that are no bigger than your fingernail!

Reefs are rocky structures that are home to little squashy polyps, which are related to sea anemones and jellyfish. The polyps use minerals from the water to create rocky cups around themselves. Over many years, thousands of polyps add to a reef, and it grows bigger. Lots of other animals find refuge in the reef and become part of a precious ecosystem. Polyps grow best in warm, shallow, and clean water in the tropics just north and south of the Equator.

Many of the species living in reefs look like plants, but are animals that feed on fish and animal scraps.

400 species of coral make up the Great Barrier Reef.

Around 1,500 species of fish live on the Great Barrier Reef.

The world's largest reef is the Great Barrier Reef, which runs some 1,250 miles along the eastern coast of Australia and covers an area of about 80,000 square miles.

Reef-building corals need sunlight and cannot live below about 200 feet. They are also very sensitive to water temperature and cannot tolerate changes of more than about 1.8°F. Coral polyps can be as small as 0.1 inches, but they form colonies up to 60 inches across.

Hideaways

Many reef-dwellers use camouflage to keep them safe in the sea. They may choose bright colors and hide in the coral itself, or disguise themselves with sandy colors to burrow into the seabed.

COMMON OCTOPUS

Ripley's Believe It or Not!®

Toothy monsters

Moray eels cannot swallow their prey. Instead, they have a second set of teeth in their throat, which move forward to grab the prey and pull it into their body to digest.

DIVE IN!

Coral reefs are very fragile, and each year boat propellers, anchors, fishing nets, and careless divers damage large areas of reef.

Beware of the attractive red fire coral—if touched with bare skin the coral polyps will deliver a nasty sting.

Coral reefs sometimes form ring-shaped islands, known as atolls, around the craters of undersea volcanoes.

The shallow waters off Palm Beach, Florida, are home to an unusual reef: an artificial commemorative reef, made from concrete cases containing the cremated remains of dead people.

The Great Barrier Reef is longer than the west coast of the USA.

twist it!

Cleaning up

Certain small fish have an important job on the reef—cleaning up. Larger fish allow them to swim into their mouth, without eating them, to nibble at the parasites that pester them. Some turtles visit special "cleaning stations" to get rid of unwanted hitchhikers on their shells and soft undersides.

ON THE EDGE

COASTLINES

Coasts are the world's most popular places to live, but they are also among the most dangerous. Crashing waves, storm surges, collapsing cliffs, and terrible tsunamis mark out the seashore as a place of potential peril!

The ebb and flow of tides also make their mark on coastal life and landforms. Twice a day, the water level at a shore rises and falls in a freaky phenomenon we call tides.

High tides and low tides are the result of big bulges in seawater that are caused by the Moon! As our near neighbor orbits Earth, and Earth spins, the Moon's gravity pulls on the water, forcing it to move in and out at coastlines.

Many mountaineers climb up the stack to reach the top.

The Old Man of Hoy is still being eroded and getting weaker at its base.

This tall rock is called the Old Man of Hoy. It is 449 feet high and is found in the Orkney Islands, Scotland. Rocks like this one are called sea stacks and are made when the waves crash against the coast. Eventually enough rock is worn away to leave a tower standing on its own.

The rock was probably part of the coast as little as 400 years ago.

Along steep rocky coasts, the action of the tide and waves often forms vertical cliffs. The world's tallest sea cliffs are on Canada's Baffin Island and rise some 4,500 feet above the sea.

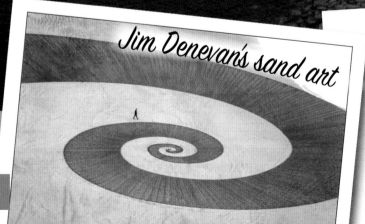

Jim Denevan's sand art

Sand artist Jim Denevan spends up to 7 hours creating his pictures. He uses a stick washed up from the sea to draw with, and walks up to 30 miles up and down the beach. When the waves come, his work is washed away.

FIX STAMP HERE

P. Mariner

Lighthouse Road

Norfolk

twist it!

Alaska's coastline is longer than the coastlines of every other US state added together.

Fjords—long, narrow, and steep-sided coastal inlets—were formed when rising sea levels flooded river valleys.

The tallest wave to batter the coast appeared in July 1958 and hit the shores of Lituya Bay in Alaska. The wave was 1,720 feet high.

The sand at the Hawaiian beach of Barking Sands does actually make a noise like a dog! The dry grains of sand make a strange barking sound when you walk on it barefoot.

BAY WATCH

The greatest difference between high and low tide is found in the Bay of Fundy in Canada, where the sea rises and falls as much as 56 feet twice daily.

SAY WHAT?

The surface of the Earth can be eroded—worn away by wind, water (such as waves or rain), and ice.

Around 11 billion cubic feet of sand have been used to make the islands.

Ripley's—— Believe It or Not!®

This set of 300 islands has been created in the sea, 4 miles from Dubai's coast. Sand was pumped from the shallow waters and used to build new land in the shape of many of the world's countries. You can buy your own island for a minimum price of $15 million!

The World islands were started in 2003. Three palm islands have also been built nearby.

Dan Belcher's sand sculptures

Beaches are formed along gently sloping coastlines where the waves deposit sand, pebbles, and even crushed coral, which have been washed away from other parts of the coastline. Sand is made up of tiny grains of crushed and decomposed rocks, shells, and coral.

FIX STAMP HERE

David Jones

Beach Drive

Coastville West

29

COOL WATERS

RIVERS, WATERFALLS, AND LAKES

Water, water, everywhere! Get the umbrella out and put your boots on—more than 121,000 cubic miles of water is expected to fall on Earth in the next year.

Thirsty plants will suck up most of it to make food, but about one third will flow, in streams and rivers, back to the sea. The source of a river is usually high in the mountains, and the water flows downward fast; full of energy, it carves valleys into the rock. By the time a river reaches its mouth, it's worn itself out and flows more slowly, depositing sand, mud, and silt in a flood plain, as it meanders toward the sea.

Niagara Falls are the most powerful waterfalls in North America.

>>Fall guy<<

The first person to walk across Niagara Falls on a tightrope was Jean-Francois Gravelet, also known as "The Great Blondin," of France. In 1859, he used a 1,100-foot rope and walked from bank to bank, dressed in a wig, purple vest, and pantaloons. He also crossed on a bicycle, in the dark, on stilts, carrying a man on his back, with a wheelbarrow, and on one trip he carried a table and stopped in the middle to eat cake.

The falls are separated by Goat Island.

There are two waterfalls on the Niagara River: Horseshoe Falls and the American Falls.

Take a drop

Niagara Falls, on the US—Canadian border, are unusually wide, with terrific amounts of water flowing over them. If temperatures drop low enough, an ice bridge may form across the river.

Amazing Amazon

The world's mightiest river is the Amazon, which flows for 3,990 miles across South America. Enough fresh water pours from the Amazon into the Atlantic Ocean every day to provide the USA with the water it needs for five months–ten times the amount of water carried by the Mississippi River.

At its widest point, the Amazon is 6.8 miles wide during the dry season. During the rainy season, it grows to around 24.8 miles across. Where the Amazon opens at its estuary, the river is over 202 miles wide!

Going to great lengths

Slovenian Martin Strel has swum some of the world's greatest rivers. His most amazing achievement, in 2007, saw him swim the length of the Amazon River in only 66 days. He had to swim for up to 12 hours each day to cover the distance, in muddy waters that hide flesh-eating fish, poisonous spiders, and dangerous snakes, wearing a homemade mask to protect his face against sunburn.

twist it!

The world's largest lake is the Caspian Sea, which borders Russia, Iran, and Turkmenistan, with a total area of about 143,000 square miles.

An incredible sight was reported at Florida's Gasparilla Lake in August 2003. Despite the lake being totally landlocked, with no links to the sea, locals saw a dolphin swimming there!

In the southwestern USA, the Colorado River has slowly cut down through solid rock to create the 277-mile-long Grand Canyon, which has an average depth of 4,060 feet.

Mountain streams in Valais, Switzerland, are home to hungry snakes, which lie in wait and grab trout that jump above the water.

The world's longest river is the Nile, which flows 4,132 miles from Lake Victoria in central Africa to the Mediterranean Sea.

HIGH AND FLOW

BIG WORD ALERT

MEANDER
To follow a winding path–like a river does as it nears the sea.

Lakes are temporary gatherings of water that have not found their way to the sea.

Waterfalls are made where hard rock forms part of the riverbed. The flowing water cannot erode the hard rock, but does wear away the soft rock around it, forming a step in the river where the water drops over the edge.

31

RIVERS OF ICE

A glacier is a vast body of frozen water that flows downhill, like a river. There's one important difference though—glaciers move sooooo slooooowly that you could sit and stare at one for ages, and not spot any change.

When a glacier moves, its great weight melts the ice at its bottom, so it actually glides along on a thin film of water, like an ice skater. These rivers of ice are big and tough. Glaciers grind away at rocks, creating U-shaped valleys and collecting a heavy load of rocks and pebbles. When a glacier melts, piles of pebbles might be one of the few signs that i ever existed!

DANGER ZONE

Cracks in a glacier, called crevasses, can be deeper than 100 feet and have steep, straight sides. Mountaineers must take care not to fall into them. That sounds easy, but sometimes a crevasse can be hidden by a snow bridge that looks safe to walk across.

SLOW MOTION

Glaciers move very, very slowly. A glacier that travels a mile in a month is considered to be moving at high speed. Each snowfall adds another layer to a glacier's surface and increases the pressure on the ice beneath. The ice at the bottom of a glacier is so compressed that it looks blue.

This beautiful, crystal-clear pool on top of a glacier is water, not ice. The sun gets hot enough to melt the surface snow and ice and create a pool on top of the frozen layer.

SO COOL

On Greenland and Antarctica, there is so much ice, and so many glaciers, that they have joined together into vast "seas" of ice that are known as ice-sheets.

Some mountain glaciers in European ski resorts are wrapped in reflective foil to stop them from melting in summer.

A melting iceberg makes a fizzing sound, known as "Bergie Seltzer." It is caused by trapped air bubbles that pop as they are released.

An Arctic iceberg was seen at latitude 28°22′ - that's just south of Daytona Beach in Florida.

There is a small glacier inside the crater of the extinct volcano Mount Kilimanjaro, located only 3 degrees south of the Equator in East Africa.

twist it!

CALVING

Large chunks of ice may "calve" (break away) from a glacier and float out to sea as an iceberg. Some icebergs are huge: as big and heavy as two Statues of Liberty. Smaller, car-sized icebergs are known as growlers. Blue stripes may form if the ice freezes super fast and contains no air bubbles.

Wakeboarding is a mixture of surfing, snow boarding, and water skiing. Boarders are towed along on a cable and perform jumps and tricks. In July 2008, extreme wakeboarders from Florida made the trip to the Arctic to test their skills on the enormous icebergs there.

>> Berg boarding <<

FROZEN WILDERNESS

POLAR REGIONS

The Earth's extremes are five times colder than the inside of a freezer. These poles are places where only the strongest survive.

More than 90 percent of the world's fresh water is permanently frozen into ice at the poles. Around the North Pole there is no land, only frozen water that covers around 4 million square miles in the winter. The continent of Antarctica covers the South Pole, and has an area of 5.5 million square miles. It's almost entirely buried beneath snow and ice up to nearly 3 miles thick.

SLEEPING ON ICE

Several hotels north of the Arctic Circle make the most of the freezing conditions to attract visitors. The hotels are built from ice and snow, with beds lined with reindeer fur to keep guests cosy at night. The hotels have to be rebuilt every year.

The term Arctic is derived from the Greek arktos, meaning bear. It was named for the polar bear.

The polar bear is the world's largest land predator.

Polar bears are found only in the Arctic region.

Superhuman

Lewis Gordon Pugh, a British endurance swimmer and explorer, loves the cold. In July 2007 he swam just over half a mile across the Arctic Ocean from the geographic North Pole in only 18 minutes and 50 seconds. Wearing only briefs, a cap and goggles, the temperature ranged between freezing 29°F and 32°F–brrr!

There are seven countries with parts inside the Arctic Circle: Russia, Finland, Sweden, Norway, Greenland, Canada, and the USA (Alaska). Most of the area known as the North Pole is frozen sea, not land.

NORTH POLE

Arctic Circle

Tropic of Cancer

N

NE

NW

... a country. Nobody lives there permanently. It has no cities or towns, but it does have many research stations for scientists.

The coldest recorded natural temperature was −128.6°F in Antarctica in July 1983.

>>See through<<

Wright Valley in Antarctica's McMurdo Dry Valleys is home to Lake Vanda. Parts of Lake Vanda are warm and unfrozen, but the ice that forms around the edge is said to be the clearest ice in the world.

SOUTH POLE

Antarctic Circle

SE

S

SW

Antarctica is the windiest place on Earth. At Commonwealth Bay, wind speed regularly reaches 200 mph.

twist it!

The lowest point on Earth's land surface is the Bentley Trench in Antarctica, and it is completely covered by ice. The bottom of the trench is more than 8,000 feet below sea level.

Bouvet Island is probably the world's most remote place. No one lives there, and it is 1,050 miles from its nearest neighbor, Queen Maud Land in Antarctica.

The foxhound was carried away to sea in a blizzard and traveled 43 miles over five days.

A dog named Scooter had to be rescued from an ice floe after chasing a coyote and becoming stranded.

US explorer Richard Byrd (1888–1957) spent six months of an Antarctic winter living alone in a shack only 9 feet by 13 feet buried beneath the snow.

GOING TO EXTREMES

Freezing sea

Sea ice grows in stages. Small ice needles get together as mushy grease ice. Waves and wind squash this into pancake ice. Gradually, the pancakes freeze together and become permanent pack ice. This can attach itself to land, or move around the ocean.

PANCAKE ICE

FASCINATING FACT! FASCINATING FACT! FASCINATING FACT!

PACK ICE

35

DRY AS A BONE
DESERTS

Water is a very precious thing in a desert. These arid places get fewer than 10 inches of rain in one year, but in reality many get far less than that. Just one inch of rain falls in Africa's Sahara Desert in an average year!

Imagine a desert and visions of golden dunes, palm-fringed oases, and cloudless skies come to mind. In fact, while some deserts have perfect fields of sand dunes, called ergs, many more are vast, windswept plains covered with stones, gravel, dried-out mud, and salt. About 8 million square miles (or 14 percent) of the Earth's land is desert, and the animals, plants, and people that live here battle for survival in one of Earth's harshest habitats.

The Sahara is the largest desert in the world. It has a total area of about 3.5 million square miles—about as big as the USA. Every year, around 700 people enter the Sand Marathon, which takes place in the Moroccan part of the desert. Competitors race 150 miles across sand dunes, through sandstorms, and in temperatures of 120°F.

Some sand dunes grow to 700 feet high.

The only deserts larger than the Sahara are cold deserts: the Arctic and the Antarctic.

The Sahara crosses 11 countries.

Desert temperatures are hot in the day but fall to below freezing at night.

Hot hideaway

The Sonoran Desert is home to the Couch's spadefoot toad. This clever creature stays underground, only emerging in July when the rainy season comes.

Ripley's Believe It or Not!®

The word "Sahara" comes from the Arabic for "desert."

BLOWN AWAY

As the wind blows across the "Empty Quarter" desert on the Arabian Peninsula, it creates sand dunes. Many dunes are crescent-shaped, but sometimes changes in wind direction form these unusual dot-shapes.

BIG WORD ALERT

WADIS
Dried up riverbeds in the desert. If it rains they fill with water and become rivers again for a short time.

Plane graveyard

The Sonoran Desert in the southwest US is home to a graveyard with a difference: it's where old planes go to die. Rows of them are kept at the Davis-Monthan Air Force Base in Tucson. The dry conditions help to preserve the planes in case they are needed for spare parts, or even to fly again.

Side step

Sidewinder snakes leave distinctive J-shaped tracks in the desert sand. They move sideways and are very fast.

Life support

An oasis is a rare place in a desert where water is close enough to the surface to form springs, streams, and small lakes. However, around three quarters of the oases in the Sahara Desert are man-made. Water is directed to chosen places to allow trees to grow, giving valuable shade from the non-stop sunshine.

Twist it!

HOT STUFF

Deserts shrink and grow in size over time—at present, the Sahara Desert is gradually expanding southward. As the Sahara Desert grew northward, toward the Mediterranean, it swallowed up hundreds of ancient Roman cities.

There are parts of the Atacama Desert in Chile where no rainfall has been recorded for more than 20 years.

The Simpson Desert in Australia is closed in summer! Authorities stop tourists from going there to allow it time to regenerate, and to prevent the many accidents and deaths that happen in the hottest months.

The camel is known as the "ship of the desert" because it can travel for days in desert conditions without eating or drinking.

PASTURES NEW

GRASSLANDS

Grass is one of nature's top success stories— it's almost indestructible! This hardy plant can survive wildfires, and being grazed, mown, frozen, scorched, trampled, and blasted by high winds.

Grass grows shoots at ground level, so even if its long, narrow leaves are damaged, it can recover. It grows where there is too little rain for trees, and too much rain for deserts to form. In warm temperate zones, grasslands are called prairies, steppes, veldts, and pampas. In the hot tropics, grasslands are called savannas and some types of savanna grasses can grow to 25 feet high.

Zebras eat only the top part of grass stalks, leaving the rest for different types of animals.

No flight zone

Ratites are a family of flightless birds that live in grassland areas of the world. The ostrich lives in Africa, the emu lives in Australia, and the rhea lives in South America. An ostrich eye measures almost 2 inches across and is as big as its brain—about the size of a walnut.

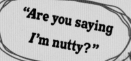

"Are you saying I'm nutty?"

Savanna is grassland with a few trees that provide valuable food and shade for animals.

Mighty mound

The savanna is home to huge termite mounds and acacia trees. Clay mounds of 10 feet are common, but some giants reach 30 feet high. Acacia trees provide food for many animals—even the roots are eaten by porcupines. The trees have sharp thorns to protect them, but a giraffe's tongue is so leathery it can eat the leaves without feeling pain.

HOME ON THE RANGE

In 1800, the prairies of North America were home to herds of wild bison (buffalo) that contained up to 30 million animals. In 2010, the Bridges family house in Texas is home to a single buffalo called Wildthing! He is allowed into their house, except when he is in a bad mood, when his 2,000-pound bulk makes him too dangerous to live in a small space.

MUCHAS GRASSES

The elephant grass that grows on the savannas of India can reach 25 feet in height.

A large swarm of locusts can strip an area of grassland the size of 60 square miles—twice the size of Manhattan—in a day, eating about 20,000 tons of vegetation.

The savannas in the cerrado region of Brazil and Paraguay are home to about 5 percent of the world's animal species.

Savannas have long, dry winters with about 4 inches of rain, and shorter summers with up to 25 inches of rain each month.

twist it!

Natural grasslands cover nearly 4 million square miles of Earth's surface.

>> Hiding space <<

When baobab trees lose their leaves in the dry season they look as if they are stuck upside down in the ground! The massive trunk becomes hollow as the tree gets older. These hollow spaces have been made into homes, chapels, a post office, a pub, and even a toilet!

WILD WOODLANDS

CONIFEROUS AND TEMPERATE FORESTS

Life is harsh near the North Pole, and plants struggle to survive when temperatures drop. Conifer trees, however, can cope with the cold, and grow in enormous forests that stretch around the globe. Also known as needle-leaf trees, conifers cover around 6.4 million square miles through North America, Europe, and Asia.

Moving south, the weather warms up. Here in the wet and mild temperate zone deciduous trees grow and create a habitat for woodland life such as deer and foxes. When winter approaches, the trees lose their leaves, settle down for a long nap, and wait for spring.

The Siberian larch is probably the world's most widespread conifer.

The trees' sap contains "antifreeze" so water inside the tree doesn't freeze.

Coniferous trees have thin needle-shaped leaves that generally remain on the tree throughout the year. They do not have flowers, but produce their seeds inside cones. These open in dry weather so that the seeds can be blown away by the wind, and close in damp conditions to keep the seeds safe.

Nature's giant

The largest single living thing on Earth is a coniferous tree. The Giant Sequoia known as "General Sherman" in California is nearly 275 feet high and weighs an estimated 2,500 tons. Usually, these trees grow to at least 165 feet: the height of 40 ten-year-olds standing on top of each other!

CONIFEROUS

SPRING

SUMMER

FALL

WINTER

Green, Amber, Red

Deciduous trees go through a yearly cycle. In spring and summer, buds unfurl, blossoms bloom, and the tree sports its full crowning glory of leaves. In fall, the trees start to lose their leaves ready to preserve energy in the cold winter months. Many trees are famous for their glorious fall colors of red, orange, and gold.

Around 200 petrified trees were discovered by Clyde Friend on his land in Washington State. The forest contained maple, elm, hickory, and sweetgum trees, and was preserved over 15 million years ago when it was covered by lava.

A sycamore tree in Scotland has "swallowed" a bicycle that was left against it for years, and grown around the metal with its trunk.

Miners in Hungary in 2007 were digging for coal but found instead an eight-million-year-old forest! The 16 trees they discovered were all fossilized but were still wood, instead of turning to stone as trees often do when buried.

Siberia contains 20 percent of the world's forests, and 50 percent of the world's coniferous forests.

TREE TIME!

A 200-year-old chestnut tree in Dorset, England, had to be chopped down in 2007 because of wood rot. Amazingly, the tree surgeons found the image of a tree in one of the branches! The shape was caused by the disease in the wood.

DECIDUOUS

The root of the problem

A pine tree stump in Michigan has been left high and dry by erosion. The tree was felled and after 40 years of being blown by the wind, the roots were left exposed 6 feet above the ground.

Tree people

This man is actually a living, growing tree! He was created by Peter and Becky Cook of Queensland, Australia. They carefully grow and graft trees into their chosen design, and have also made a growing chair strong enough for you to sit on.

STEAMY SURROUNDINGS

TROPICAL RAINFORESTS

Trekking through a warm, wet tropical rainforest is tough. Enormous trees, hanging vines, and large, lush leaves fill every available space and it can be a battle to make any headway.

Rainforests contain a bigger range of animals and plants than anywhere else on Earth. Just 1 acre might contain up to 120 different types of tree. Because the rainforest floor is dark, the trees have tall, straight trunks so their upper branches can reach the sunlight, and create a canopy 150 feet high.

twist it!

GREEN SCENE

The tallest rainforest trees are known as emergents because they emerge above the canopy. In Sarawak, Malaysia, the species *Koompassia excelsa* grows to heights of more than 262 feet.

The rainforest talipot palm blooms with over 20 million individual flowers.

A quarter of the medicines we have today owe their existence to rainforest plants.

The canopy trees are packed so closely together that it can take ten minutes for rain to get through and reach the ground.

Several rainforest frogs use their bright colors to warn off hungry predators. Certain species ooze poison through their skin. Many are called "poison dart frogs," as some rainforest tribes were said to smear the poison on the tips of their darts for hunting—although they are far more likely to use poisonous plants for this.

The hot lips plant has special leaves that look—you guessed it—just like bright red lips. It grows in the rainforests of Ecuador in South America.

The Rafflesia plant of the Sumatran rainforest bears a single flower that measures up to 3½ feet in diameter and smells like rotting meat.

THE WANDERER

The wandering spider lives in Brazil, and is responsible for more human deaths than any other spider. This one is eating a termite. Their name comes from their habit of wandering through the forest rather than making webs.

The monkey slug caterpillar has pairs of hairy "legs" that make it look more like a tarantula than a caterpillar. Underneath, it has normal legs, body, and head. The fake legs can sting for added protection.

HAIRY SCARY

Larger than life

Tropical rainforests cover about 4.4 million square miles of the Earth's surface. The largest is the Amazon rainforest with an area of about 2.3 million square miles, across nine countries. More than half the world's rainforests are found in just three countries: Brazil, Democratic Republic of the Congo, and Indonesia.

The longest stick insects in the world live in the rainforests of Borneo and can be 20 inches long. Many rainforest species grow extremely large. The titan beetle of the Amazonian rainforest (see below) is one of the biggest insects in the world, reaching lengths of 6½ inches.

Actual size!

43

EARTH IN DANGER

TIME IS RUNNING OUT

Twenty thousand years ago the Earth was in the grip of an Ice Age, and massive sheets of ice reached as far south as London and New York. Since then, the world has been slowly but gradually getting warmer.

The Earth's climate has been changing for billions of years; sometimes it's hotter than today, sometimes it's colder. However, scientists believe that the global warming we are experiencing now is not just a natural phenomenon. It's thought we humans are making it worse by putting more carbon dioxide (CO_2) gas in the atmosphere, by burning fossil fuels.

Man-made climate change is having such an effect on the world's plants and animals that a quarter of all species could die out in years, not centuries. Some scientists suggest that Australia could lose more than half of its types of butterfly by 2050.

Going under

The city of New Orleans is on the shifting delta of the Mississippi River, and its highest point is only 6 feet above sea level. Its residents have always lived in fear of hurricanes and flooding. Now scientists are warning that rising sea levels will surround the city and cut it off from the mainland, probably within 100 years.

Hurricane Katrina in 2005 caused over 125 billion dollars-worth of damage and left tens of thousands of people with no home.

Heating up

Global warming has one certain effect: ice begins to melt. At both poles, the ice sheets are getting smaller. Large chunks fall into the sea. Scientists have recorded rising sea levels of about 0.1 in each year, and are worried that they may be 3 feet higher by the end of the century.

44

>>Chopped down<<

Massive parts of the world's rainforests are being cut down to make room for farms and roads, and to provide timber. An area of rainforest the size of two soccer pitches is destroyed every second. This leaves local people, and some of the world's rarest animal species, with nowhere to live.

>>Bottles banked<<

Not everyone throws away their trash. Maria Ponce of El Salvador has built a whole house out of empty plastic bottles!

SAY WHAT?

Mount Rumpke is the highest point in Hamilton County, Ohio, (1,000 feet) and is completely made of garbage.

Filling up

Our planet is getting full: full of people, homes, farms, cars, cities... we're running out of space. The more people crowd onto our planet, the harder it is for the Earth to supply the food, fuel, and land we need. One billion people (a sixth of the world's population) live in shanty towns, which are made up of thousands of shelters built from scraps, squashed into dangerously small, unhealthy spaces.

Thrown away

More people make more waste. We now know that it's better to reuse whatever we can, instead of filling our trash or making new things. Burying our rubbish underground can be bad for the environment, and producing new cars, TVs, and all the items we use in modern life takes up valuable energy and materials.

EXTREME EARTH INDEX

Bold numbers refer to main entries; numbers in *italic* refer to the illustrations

A

acacia trees *38*, 39
Adams, Warren and Pam 23, *23*
air **20–21**
airplanes, stored in desert 37, *37*
Alaska 29
Alps 17
Alvin, US 25
Amazon rainforest 43
Amazon River 31
animals 6
   and climate change 44
   on grasslands 38–39
   in rainforests 42
Antarctica **34–35**, 36
Appalachian Mountains 13
Arabian Peninsula 37
Arctic 16, **34**, 36
Atacama Desert 37
Atlantic Ocean 24, 31
atmosphere 6, **20–21**, 44
atolls 27
auroras 20, *20*
axis 6, 7

B

Baffin Island 16, *16*, 28
baobab trees 39, *39*
Barking Sands, Hawaii 29
basalt 16, *16*
beaches 28, 29, *29*
beetles 19, *19*, 43, *43*
Belcher, Dan 29, *29*
Bentley Trench, Antarctica 35
"Bergie Seltzer" 33
bicycle, swallowed by tree 41
birds, in grasslands 38
bison 39, *39*
blackwater rafting 19
Blondin, Charles 30, *30*
boat, bottle-shaped 24
bottles, house built of 45, *45*
Bouvet Island 35
buffalo 39, *39*
Byrd, Richard 35

C

Caledonian Mountains 13
camels 37
camouflage 27, *27*
carbon dioxide 44
Caspian Sea 31
caterpillars 43, *43*
Cauldwell, Ray 22
caves **18–19**
Central America, volcanoes 15
China, earthquakes 11, *11*
cirrus clouds 20, *20*
clay 16

cliffs 28, *28*
climate 20
climate change **44–45**
clouds 20, *20*
coal mines 18, 41
coasts **28–29**
Colorado River 31
Columbus, Christopher 24
condensation 21, *21*
coniferous forests 40–41
continents 8
Coober Pedy, Australia 19, *19*
Cook, Mount 12
Cook, Peter and Becky 41, *41*
coral reefs **26–27**
core, Earth's 8, *8*
Cotapaxi 15
Coyote Buttes 16, *16–17*
craters, volcanoes 8, 9, 33
Crazy Horse, Chief 13
crevasses 32, *32*
crust, Earth's **8–9**, 16
crystals 18, *18*

D

days 6, 7
Death Valley 13
deciduous trees 40, 41, *41*
Denevan, Jim 28, *28*
deserts **36–37**
dinner party, on mountain 12, 13, *13*
diving 24
dog, stranded on ice floe 35
dolphin, in lake 31
Dorje Sherpa, Pem 13
dormant volcanoes 14
Dubai 29, *29*
dunes 36, 37
dust, space 21

E

earthquakes 8, 9, **10–11**
ecosystems, coral reefs 26
El Paso Mountains 19
electricity, in lightning storms 22
elements 16
elephant grass 39
"Empty Quarter", Arabian Peninsula 37
emus 38
Enukso Point, Baffin Island 16, *16*
epicenter, earthquake 10
erosion 12, 18, 28, 29
eruptions, volcanoes 14, 15, *15*
evaporation 21, *21*
Everest, Mount 7, 12, *12*, 13, 19

F

fangtooth fish 24, *24*
fault lines 9
fireflies 19, *19*
fish
   coral reefs 26–27, *26–27*
   in hurricanes 23, *23*
   in oceans 24, *24*
   predicting earthquakes 11
fjords 29
flood plains 30
floods 23
forests **40–41**
fossil fuels 44
fossils 7, *7*, 17, *17*, 41
Friend, Clyde 41
frogs 42, *42*
Fundy, Bay of 29
fungi 7, *7*, 17, *17*

G

galaxies 6
gales 22
garbage 45
gases, in atmosphere **20–21**
Gasparilla Lake, Florida 31
gems 16
"General Sherman" sequoia 40, *40*
geologists 17
Giant's Causeway 16, *16*
glaciers 12, 17, **32–33**
global warming **44–45**
Grand Canyon 31
grasslands **38–39**
gravity, tides 28
Great Barrier Reef 26, *26*, 27
growlers 33
gypsum 18, *18*

H

hailstones 20, *20*
"hairy" rock 17, *17*
Hawaii
   Barking Sands 29
   rainfall 21
   volcanoes 15, *15*
Hegarty, Margaret 9
Himalayas 12, 13
hot lips plant 42, *42*
hotel, ice 34, *34*
humans, early 6, *6*
hurricanes 23, 44
hydrothermal vents 25, *25*

I

ice 23, *23*
   erosion 12, 29
   glaciers **32–33**
   global warming **44**, 44
   ice sheets 33, **44**
   icebergs 33, *33*
   poles **34–35**
Ice Age 44

igneous rocks 16
International Space Station 15
"inukshuk" (stone landmarks) 16, *16*
Irazu, Mount 24
islands
   artificial 29, *29*
   coral atolls 27

J

Japan, earthquakes 10, *10*
jellyfish 24, *24*

K

K2 12
Kanuha, CJ 15, *15*
Kilauea volcano 14, *14*
Kilimanjaro, Mount 33
kingdoms, living things 6
Kobe earthquake 10, *10*
Koster, Patrick 9
Krakatoa 14

L

lakes 24, **30–31**
Latin names 6
lava 8, 9, 14, 15, 41
Libbrecht, Kenneth 22, *22*
life **6–7**
light, from Sun 6–7
lightning 22, *22*
limestone 17, 18
Lituya Bay, Alaska 29
locusts 39

M

McClean, Tom 24
McMurdo Dry Valleys, Antarctica 35
magma 8, 9, 15, 16, 25
Mammoth Cave complex 19, *19*
mantle, Earth's 8, *8*, 9
marathons
   in deserts 36, *36–37*
   running on every continent 9
marble 17
Mauna Loa 15
meanders 30, 31
metamorphic rocks 16, 17
Mexico
   earthquakes 11
   volcanoes 15
Mexico, Gulf of 19
Milky Way 6
minerals **16–17**, 26
mines 18, *18*, 41
Mississippi River 31, 44, *44*
molecules, in water 24
monera 7, *7*
monkey slug caterpillar 43, *43*
Moon, effect on tides 28
Moray eels 27, *27*
Morrow, Pat 12
mountains 8, **12–13**, 17, 30
mud baths 14, *14*

Mulepati, Mona 13
mushrooms 7

N
Naica Mine, Mexico 18, *18*
names, Latin 6
Native Americans, memorial to
13, *13*
Nereus (robotic sub) 25, *25*
New Orleans 44–45, *44–45*
Niagara Falls 30, *30*
Nile, River 31
North Pole **34**, 40
Northern Lights 20, *20*

O
oases 37, *37*
oceans **24–25**
    coasts **28–29**
    Panthalassa 8, *8*
octopuses 25, *25*, 27, *27*
oil wells 19
Old Man of Hoy 28, *28–29*
orbit, Earth around Sun 6,
    7
organisms 6
ostriches 38, *38*
oxygen 9, 16

P
Pacific Ocean 21, 24
pack ice 35, *35*
Palm Beach, Florida 27
palm trees 42
pampas 38
pancake ice 35, *35*
Pangaea 8, *8*
Panthalassa 8, *8*
petrified trees 41
pine trees 40, 41
planets 6
plants 6
    and climate change 44
    forests **40–41**
    grasslands **38–39**
    in rainforests 42
    water and 30
plate tectonics **8–9**
    earthquakes 10
    mountain building 12, 13,
        13
    volcanoes 15
"poison dart frogs" 42,
    42
polar bears 34, *34*
poles **34–35**, 44
polyps, coral 26
Pompeii 15, *15*
Ponce, Maria 45, *45*
population 45
prairies 38, 39
precipitation 21, *21*
protista 7, *7*
Pugh, Lewis 34, *34*
pumice stones 15

R
rabbit, volcano 15
radioactivity 9
radium 9
Rafflesia plant 42, *42*
rafting, blackwater 19
rain 22
    in deserts 36, 37
    erosion 29
    in grasslands 38, 39
    water cycle 20, 21, *21*
rainbows 21
rainforests **42–43**, 45
ratites 38
recycling 45
reefs **26–27**
rheas 38
Richter Scale 11
rift valleys 8
rivers 24, **30–31**
    underground rivers 18
robotic sub 25, *25*
rocks **16–17**
    caves **18–19**
    coasts **28–29**
    crust **8–9**
    erosion 12
    fossils 7, *7*
    glaciers and 32
    magma 9, 15
    volcanoes 14
    waterfalls 31
rubbish 45
Rumpke, Mount 45

S
Sahara Desert 21, 36, *36*,
    37
salt water 24
San Andreas Fault 9
San Francisco earthquake 11,
    11
sand 28, 29
sand art 28, *28*, 29, *29*
sand dunes 36, 37
Sand Marathon 36, *36–37*
sandstone 16, *16–17*
Sarychev Peak 15, *15*
savannas 38–39, *38–39*
Schmidt, William 19
Scots pine 40
scuba diving 24
sea ice 35, *35*
sea stacks 28, *28*
seas **24–5**, 30
    coasts **28–29**
    sea level rises **44**
seasons 7, *7*
sedimentary rocks 16, *16–17*
seismographs 10, *10*
sequoias 40, *40*
Seven Summits 12
shale 17
shanty towns 45, *45*

sharks 24, *24*
shock waves, earthquakes 11
Siberia 41
sidewinder snakes 37, *37*
Simpson Desert 37
slate 17
snakes
    in deserts 37, *37*
    in earthquakes 11
    in mountain streams 31
snow 21, 32, 34
    snow rollers *22–23*, 23
    snowflakes 22, *22*
soccer team, killed by lightning
    22
Sonoran Desert 37, *37*
South Pole **34–35**
Southern Lights 20, *20*
space dust 21
spadefoot toad 36, *36*
speleology 19
sperm whales 25, *25*
spiders 43, *43*
spinning, Earth 7, *7*
squid 25
stalactites and stalagmites 18
Stanford, Mike 23
stars 6
Stepanek, Martin 24
steppes 38
stick insects 43, *43*
stingray 27
storms
    hurricanes 23, 44
    storm surges 22, 28
    thunderstorms 21, 22, *22*
Strel, Martin 31, *31*
submarine 25, *25*
submersibles 25
summits, mountains 12, 13
Sun 6, 6, 7, *7*, 20, 21
surfing, near volcanoes 15, *15*
swimming, in rivers 31

T
talipot palm 42
temperate forests **40–41**, 42
temperatures
    in caves 19
    climate change **44–45**
    cold weather 22
    coral reefs 26
    in deserts 36
    inside the Earth 8
    lava 14, 15
    in polar regions 34, 35
    in troposphere 21
termite mounds 38, 39
thunderstorms 21, 22, *22*
Tiber oil well 19
tidal waves 22
tides 28, 29
tightrope walking, across Niagara
    Falls 30, *30*
Titan beetle 43, *43*

toads, in deserts 36, *36*
tornados 21, *21*
Totumo volcano 14, *14*
trees 40–41, **42–43**
tropics 26, 38, **42–43**
troposphere 20, 21
tsunamis 14, 28
tunnels 18, 19
turtles 27, *27*

U
Universe 6

V
valleys 30, 32
Vanda, Lake 35
veldts 38
Vesuvius, Mount 15, *15*
volcanoes **14–15**
    coral atolls 27
    craters 9, **9**
    glacier in crater 33
    igneous rocks 16
    metamorphic rocks 17
    plate tectonics 8

W
wadis 37
Waialeale, Mount 21
wakeboarding 33, *33*
wandering spiders 43,
    43
waste 45
water
    in atmosphere 20, 21, *21*, 22
    in deserts 36, 37, *37*
    erosion 12, 18, 29
    lakes **30–31**
    and life 6
    oceans **24–25**
    rivers **30–31**
    tides 28
    waterfalls **30–31**
Wave, The, Coyote Buttes 16,
    16–17
waves 28, 29
weather 20, **22–23**
    in forests 40
    in grasslands 39
weathering 12
whales 7, 25, *25*
Whitney, Mount 13
winds
    in Antarctica 35
    erosion 29
    gales 22
    hurricanes 23
    tornados 21, *21*
woodlands **40–41**
Wright Valley, Antarctica 35

Z
Zabriskie Point 13
zebras 38–39, *38–39*

ACKNOWLEDGMENTS

COVER (sp) © Tanguy de Saint Cyr/Fotolia.com, (c) © Andrew Evans/iStock.com; **2** (b) Action Press/Rex Features, (t) Patrick Landmann/ Science Photo Library; **3** Dan Belcher www.ampersandworkshop.com; **4** (b/l) © Andrew Evans/iStock.com; **4–5** (t) ©Suzannmeer.com/ Fotolia.com; **5** (b) Yang Fan/ChinaFotoPress/Photocome/Press Association Images; **6** (b) © Eric Isselée/Fotolia.com, (b/c) AFP/Getty Images, (b/r) © iStock.com; **6–7** (dps) © Srecko Djarmati/Fotolia.com; **7** (t/l, t, t/r, b/l, b, b/r) © iStock.com; **8** (c) © Lorelyn Medina/ Fotolia.com, (b) Mikkel Juul Jensen/Bonnier Publications/Science Photo Library, (b/r) Patrick Koster/Barcroft Media Ltd; **8–9** © Jan Rysavy/iStock.com; **9** (t/r) David Parker/Science Photo Library, (b) Patrick Koster/Barcroft Media Ltd; **10** (sp) Reuters/Masaharu Hatano, (t/r) © iStock.com; **11** (t/l) Sipa Press/Rex Features, (b/r) Stringer Shanghai/Reuters, (b/c) Photolibrary.com; **12** (b) © Peter McBride/ Aurora Photos/Corbis; **12–13** (dps) Ethel Davies/Robert Harding/Rex Features, (b) Camera Press; **13** (b, b/r) Sergio Pitamitz/Robert Harding/Rex Features; **14** (b) Alex Sudea/Rex Features; **14–15** (sp) Marco Fulle/GB/Barcroft Media; **15** ((b/c) I.B.L./Rex Features, (b/r) Image Courtesy of the Image Science & Analysis Laboratory, NASA Johnson Space Center, (t/r) Kirk Lee Aeder/Barcroft Media Ltd; **16** (l) © iStock.com; (b) © Shaun Lowe/iStock.com **16–17** (c) © Surpasspro/Fotolia.com; **17** (sp) Dr Juerg Alean/Science Photo Library, (t/r) Yang Fan/ChinaFotoPress/Photocome/Press Association Images; **18** (sp) Javier Trueba/Msf/Science Photo Library; **19** (sp) © Cathy Keifer/Fotolia.com, (c) Brian Brake/Science Photo Library, (t/r) Gary Berdeaux/AP/Press Association Images, (b/r) Sam Tinson/Rex Features; **20** (t) © Usefulebooks4u/Fotolia.com, (c) © Tom Bean/Corbis, (b) Alan Blacklock NIWA; **20–21** (sp) © Bsilvia/Fotolia.com; (t) © Stas Perov/Fotolia.com, (b) © Kimberly Kilborn/Fotolia.com; **21** (b/r) © Eric Nguyen/Corbis; **22** (t) © Dan Lockard/Fotolia.com, (b) Kenneth Libbrecht/Barcroft Media; **22–23** Mike Stanford WSDOT; **23** (t) Action Press/Rex Features (c) Photograph by Ray Asgar www. austinhelijet.com, (b) Eric Gay/AP/Press Association Images; **24** (b) © iStock.com, (t/l) Michael Patrick O'Neill/Science Photo Library, (t/r) Norbert Wu/Minden Pictures/FLPA; **25** (b/l) Barcroft Media via Getty Images, (c, t/r) © NHPA/Photoshot, (b/r) Christopher Griner, Woods Hole Oceanographic Institution; **26–27** (b, dps) © iStock.com; **27** (c) © Doug Perrine/naturepl.com, (t/l) Georgette Douwma/ Science Photo Library, (t/r) © David Fleetham/naturepl.com; **28** (sp) © David Woods/iStock.com, (b) Jim Denevan; **29** (b/l) Dan Belcher www.ampersandworkshop.com, (t/r) Reuters/Anwar Mirza, (r) Reuters/Ho New; **30** (b/l) Getty Images; **30–31** Hans-Peter Merten; **31** (l) www.amazonswim.com; **32** (l) © iStock.com, (r) Roberto Rinaldi/Bluegreenpictures.com; **33** (l) © Martin Harvey/Corbis, (b/r) Christian Pondella/Barcroft Media Ltd, (t/r) © iStock.com; **34** (sp) Larry Broder, (b/l) Kev Cunnick, (t/r) Ho New/Reuters; **34–35** © iStock.com; **35** (sp) Geoff Renner, (b/l) © iStock.com, (b/c) © Staphy/Fotolia.com, (t/r) George Steinmetz/Science Photo Library; **36** (sp) AFP/Getty Images, (b/r) Rodger Jackman; **37** (t/l) © George Steinmetz/Corbis, (t/r) Getty Images, (c) © NHPA/Photoshot, (b) © BasPhoto/Fotolia. com; **38** (b/l) © Irina Igumnova/iStock.com, (t/r) © Nyiragongo/Fotolia.com; **38–39** © Markus Divis/iStock.com; **39** (t) Sherron Bridges, (c) Photolibrary.com, (b) © iStock.com; **40** (sp) © Marco Maccarini/iStock.com, (b/l) © Dmitry Naumov/Fotolia.com, (b/c) © Fantasista/ Fotolia.com, (b/r) © Urosr/Fotolia.com; **41** (sp) © Stephan Levesque/iStock.com, (t/l) © iStock.com, (tr) © Olga Shelego/Fotolia.com, (t/bl) © Rxr3rxr3/Fotolia.com, (t/br) © Sean Gladwell/Fotolia.com, (c) Bournemouth News & Pic Service/Rex Features, (b/r) Pooktre. com; **42** (l) © iStock.com, (b/c) Dr Morley Read/Science Photo Library, (b/r) © Dejan Suc/iStock.com; **42–43** (dps) © iStock.com; **43** (t/l) Dr Morley Read/Science Photo Library, (t/r) © Pete Oxford/naturepl.com, (r) Hunter Stark by Tanja Stark (photographer), (b/r) Patrick Landmann/Science Photo Library; **44** (l) © PSD Photography/Fotolia.com; **44–45** (c) David J. Phillip/AP/Press Association Images; **45** (c) © Alberto L. Pomares G./iStock.com, (r) Phil Noble/PA Archive/Press Association Images, (t/r) AFP/Getty Images

Key: t = top, b = bottom, c = center, l = left, r = right, sp = single page, dp = double page, bgd = background

All other photos are from Ripley Entertainment Inc. All artwork by Rocket Design (East Anglia) Ltd.

Every attempt has been made to acknowledge correctly and contact copyright holders and we apologize in advance for any unintentional errors or omissions, which will be corrected in future editions.